# Lifelines
## Intervention

### Helping Students
### At Risk For Suicide

Maureen Underwood, L.C.S.W.
Judith Springer, Psy.D.
Michelle Ann-Rish Scott, M.S.W., Ph.D.
Society for the Prevention of Teen Suicide

HAZELDEN®

**Hazelden**
Center City, Minnesota 55012
hazelden.org

© 2011 by Hazelden Foundation
All rights reserved. Published 2011
Printed in the United States of America

ISBN: 978-1-61649-157-4

*Notice and Disclaimer*
This curriculum is for educational and informational purposes only and should not be considered, or used as a substitute for, professional medical/psychological advice, diagnosis, and treatment. Hazelden makes no warranty, guarantee, or promise, express or implied, regarding the effectiveness of this curriculum in the prevention of suicide in specific situations. Hazelden does not take responsibility for any loss, injury, or damage caused by using the curriculum information, and in no event shall Hazelden, its employees, or its contractors or agents be liable for any special indirect or consequential damages or any loss or damages whatsoever resulting from injury, loss of income or profits, whether in an action of contract, negligence, or other tortious action, arising in connection with the use or performance of any information contained in the curriculum or associated materials. Hazelden does not monitor and is not responsible for statements made by instructors or others, or for the quality of instruction provided in conjunction with this curriculum.

The lyrics from "Whore to a Chainsaw" by Thy Art Is Murder on page 109 are used with permission.

15 14 13 12 11      1 2 3 4 5 6

Cover design by David Spohn
Interior design and typesetting by Madeline Berglund

# Contents

...................................................................

# Acknowledgments

...................................................................................................

The competent-community focus of the *Lifelines* model parallels the wide range of acknowledgments we would like to make for help in putting this manual together.

At the individual level, our support ranged from experienced professionals like Teresa Mosley and Susan Paynter, who shared their expertise on counseling gifted students, to Aubrey Clark, social work intern at Monmouth University who helped us identify important resources that enriched the manual's content.

We are grateful as well to Pamela Foster, our editor at Hazelden Publishing, for continuing to patiently guide the *Lifelines* projects through what seem to us the intricacies of the publishing maze.

Sharon Shepherd-Levine and Bob Griffiths added their insightful creative stamp to the video elements, and we always appreciate the sensitive and thoughtful way they translate what's on the written page to the screen.

Scott Fritz of the Society for the Prevention of Teen Suicide continues, as always, to inspire us with his passionate commitment to the development of accurate and quality training and public awareness materials. We remain humbled by his dedication to the cause.

To our families, who understand the somewhat consuming nature of this project, your support is a footnote on every page.

And finally, the model we describe in the following pages would have remained simply an idea in our minds without the schools that invited us in to meet and train their resource staff and that gave us invaluable feedback that helped us create a model we feel is relevant to the mandate and the mission of schools. We especially appreciate the wonderful advisors and students in the peer program in West New York, New Jersey, who provide a shining example of how students can be an invaluable resource for positive change in schools.

# How to Use the CD-ROM

........................................................................................................

Included with this manual is a CD-ROM that contains a variety of reproducible resources for school resource staff to help implement *Lifelines Intervention*. All the documents on the CD-ROM can be printed and copied for personal use without worry of copyright infringement.

Whenever you see this icon ⌨ in the margin of the manual's pages, it means the indicated resource is located on the CD-ROM. To open the documents on the CD-ROM, you will need Adobe Reader. If you don't have Adobe Reader, you can download the software for free at www.adobe.com.

For a list of what is contained on the CD-ROM and for further instructions, please see the *Read Me First* document on the CD-ROM.

## Introduction

# We're All in This Together

*"I was in my second year as a school counselor when I got my first referral for assessment of a student that a teacher thought might be suicidal. I remembered what I had learned in graduate school about depression in adolescence, but I didn't remember any specifics about suicide risk assessment. I knew some questions to ask, but I'm sure there were others I missed. I don't know who was more anxious about the interview—the student or me!"*

*—MISSISSIPPI SCHOOL COUNSELOR*

## WHY DID WE WRITE THIS MANUAL?

There's been a trend in recent years to provide more education in schools about mental health, especially as it relates to suicide prevention. Many health curricula teach students about signs and symptoms of depression and other mental disorders. Faculty and staff may get the same type of training at presentations or in-service workshops. The *Lifelines* approach uses a different tactic. While we recognize the importance of mental health education, our slant on youth suicide prevention is broader and focuses on mental wellness rather than on mental illness.

The signature of *Lifelines* has been the establishment of a "competent school community," in which all members can identify the signs of suicide risk and know what to do in response. This book is written for school resource staff who are often called upon to intervene when there is concern about a student's potential suicide risk. Although we recognize that assessment by a community mental health professional is ultimately required with at-risk students, we also know that school staff may find themselves in a position of having to provide targeted interventions to facilitate those subsequent referrals. This manual reflects your unique role in this intervention process. Our goal is to provide you with helpful tips and resources to improve your comfort level in asking the questions that you need to ask in order to help save a life.

*Lifelines* also highlights the promotion of resilience or "protective" factors for youth—including assisting students in identifying trusted adults in their support network and teaching them that it's okay to ask for help.

There is, however, a paradox in school-based suicide prevention: when it's effective, more students are identified as being at potential risk. When the competent suicide prevention community is in action, this identification can come from a variety of sources: peers, faculty and staff, parents, or the at-risk students themselves. Whatever the source, however, a chain of events should be set in motion to create a safety net for the student. This safety net includes not just the resources of the school but also those of the community at large.

## WHAT IS *INTERVENTION?*

We believe that school-based intervention for suicide risk is three-tiered: one tier addresses early identification and assessment of at-risk students, the second makes referral to community resources for additional services, and the final tier enhances the protective factors that increase resilience and provide buffers from stress.

## WHAT IS THE SCHOOL'S ROLE IN INTERVENTION?

The safety net for at-risk students created in the school *does* include assessment and intervention grounded in sound mental health theory: identify the problem, gather relevant information, and make a referral (Granello and Granello 2007).

### The School's Role in Intervention

- Identification and Assessment
- Referral
- Enhancement of Protective Factors

And while this initial intervention is critical, its scope is limited. *Lifelines* firmly believes that schools are not mental health centers; they simply take the first step in getting students the mental health care they need from community resources. The guidelines that *Lifelines* presents for school-based interventions reflect that bias.

Referral to community-based resources for assessment and/or treatment is the second tier of intervention. Effective referrals involve both the student and the student's parents and require knowledge about community resources so that the resource is matched to the student's needs.

In regard to the final aspect of intervention in the school—the creation and support of "protective factors" for students—if a school is a competent and compassionate community for its students, protective factors will be inherent in the school's culture. These factors will include teaching students that it's okay to ask for help, engaging them in school and community activities, recognizing student accomplishments, and encouraging prosocial behavior by all school community members, including faculty and staff.

There's another reason schools should consider intervention as a part of a comprehensive suicide prevention protocol. Research has demonstrated that when schools implement student awareness curricula for suicide prevention, self- and peer-generated referrals tend to increase. However, while school resource staff can perform the "gatekeeper" function of making initial assessments and subsequent referrals to local mental health resources for further evaluation and follow-up, they are generally without specific protocols to guide them in these critical tasks. There are, for example, no clinical tools on the National Registry of Evidence-based Programs and Practices (NREPP) or the Best Practices Registry (BPR) of the Suicide Prevention Resource Center (SPRC) detail procedures to be used in schools. A standardized clinical framework that asks explicit questions about suicide risk is, of course, indicated, but what are the parameters for questioning in a school setting? What format should schools use to communicate information obtained in the school setting to local mental health treatment resources? And how can parents or guardians who may misunderstand or distrust mental health services be engaged as collaborators in the process?

The interventions in this manual build on the foundation of the competent and compassionate school community described in the *Lifelines* prevention model, as listed on NREPP. The manual adapts the training format for the assessment and management of suicide risk created by the Suicide Prevention Resource Center to the resources and limitations of school settings. The manual begins with a discussion of the historical context of suicide and an exploration of personal values and attitudes toward suicide. It then takes school resource staff through a process that includes preparing for the interview with the potentially at-risk student, gathering collateral information, and addressing specific topics in an interview format called "Tell Me More." The manual reviews techniques that can be useful with students who are challenging to interview, and it provides clear guidance in involving parents and guardians as partners in suicide prevention. It addresses specific needs presented by students who are bullied, members of sexual minorities, gifted, or in special education classes. Finally, this manual describes ways in which schools can increase protective factors that promote resiliency.

## WHAT ARE THE OBJECTIVES OF THIS MANUAL?

As you read this manual, you'll see it begins by creating a foundation of knowledge that grounds the school's role in assessment and intervention. It continues by addressing the following objectives:

1. To provide a context for contemporary societal values and attitudes about suicide by reviewing suicide from an historical perspective

2. To highlight the role of personal values and experiences in the assessment/intervention process

3. To present epidemiological information about suicide risk to facilitate early identification of at-risk students

4. To review a protocol for an assessment interview

5. To outline strategies for engaging students and parents in the assessment/referral process

6. To call attention to special categories of students who may be at elevated suicide risk

## HOW IS THIS MANUAL ORGANIZED?

This manual reflects what we have learned about the role of school-based resources from our sixty-plus years of collective experience in school settings. The chapters are structured around typical questions educators and school resource staff ask about intervention with potentially suicidal students. In addition to reviewing basic information about suicide to create a solid foundation for an intervention, the manual provides a template for the initial assessment in the school setting. We review the reasoning behind including particular questions in the assessment interview. The challenge of involving the student's parents in the referral process is discussed in detail, and the CD-ROM contains strategies for engaging parents. Sample interviews with both students and parents are included on the DVD.

While all interventions in this book are grounded in sound theory, their relevance to the school is explained and practical guidelines for implementation are suggested. This reflects another thread that runs through the entire *Lifelines* series: the usefulness of theory is in its application to real-life issues and problems. John Kalafat, coauthor of *Lifelines: A Suicide Prevention Program*, put it this way: "I may be a researcher and educator, but I'm also a pragmatist from the 'so what?' school of training. If there's not a practical reason to learn something, what's the point of teaching it?" John believed that adult learning theory was correct in its assessment that the information people learn best is relevant to their immediate work and should help them reach personal and professional goals—the "what's in it for them" application of theory to practice. Thus, each chapter contains quotations that bring life to the content and reflect its applicability to the experiences of different members of the competent school community.

Each chapter includes a list of resources related to specific content. As you will see, these are by no means exhaustive; they are resources that we have found particularly helpful. They are not meant to discourage readers from seeking additional resource material of their own. Whenever possible, Internet addresses are given to facilitate ease of access.

Each chapter in the *Lifelines Postvention* manual ended with a section called "In a Perfect World . . ." The section encouraged readers to think about the ways in which they could apply the manual's content in their schools. Each chapter in this manual concludes with a short section entitled "In Your Experience . . ." It asks readers to consider the more personal ways in which chapter content can inform their interventions.

## WHAT IS THE BOTTOM LINE?

This manual mirrors the *Lifelines* philosophy that theory is only as useful as its application. Sections of the manual can be used as immediate resources for the assessment and referral of a potentially suicidal student. The CD-ROM contains a PDF slide show that districts can use to train all resource staff in a consistent approach to assessment and referral. The notes that accompany each slide include specific references to chapter content to help you organize a training presentation that reflects fidelity to the *Lifelines* model.

# Chapter 1

## Building on a Strong Foundation: Administrative Frame of Reference

*"As the school administrator of a large, metropolitan district, I am acutely concerned about doing everything I can to educate the students in my charge in a safe, nonviolent environment. In recent years, I've felt that my ability to respond to the needs of students at risk for suicide has been compromised by students' rights activists championing the cause of student privacy. Between HIPAA and FERPA and threats of lawsuits, I feel between a rock and a hard place when I just want to do what's right for my kids."*

—*SCHOOL SUPERINTENDENT*

Schools today often find themselves in paradoxical positions. On the one hand, they seem to be held increasingly accountable for responding to the needs of students who might be at risk for suicide; on the other hand, they can be bombarded with caveats about respecting the privacy of individual students and families. Where is the balancing point? Certainly school board legal counsel can provide interpretation on a case-by-case basis, but a review of the big picture might provide some clarity for administrators and staff on the most commonly misunderstood parts of the process (Borowsky, Ireland, and Resnick 2001).

However, the role of school administration in suicide prevention and intervention is much broader than simply interpreting policies and establishing response protocols. The administration creates the foundation on which the competent

Duplicating this page is illegal. Do not copy this material without written permission from the publisher.

**7**

school community is based. The administration's commitment to the well-being of all members of the school community is bred into the culture of the school. In fact, when this doesn't occur, its absence is noted and resented by faculty and staff.

This chapter will discuss ways in which that administrative commitment should be demonstrated. We will review the components of the competent school community and focus specifically on the administrative issues that should be included in a comprehensive intervention plan.

By the end of this chapter, you will be able to

- understand the structure of a comprehensive youth suicide prevention program in a competent school community
- recognize when there is a need for formalized agreements with off-campus resources
- understand the applications of HIPAA and FERPA to the school in general and to students at risk for suicide

## WHAT ARE THE COMPONENTS OF A COMPETENT YOUTH SUICIDE PREVENTION COMMUNITY?

Perhaps the easiest way to envision this community is through the following diagram:

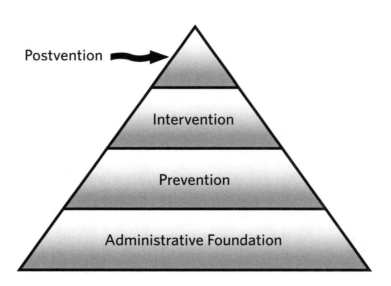

Let's start at the bottom and work our way to the top. The *administrative foundation* for the competent school community is based on the support and commitment of the school board, articulated through the principal, to policies and procedures that address the range of needs presented by students who might be at risk for suicide. In most schools, these policies address protocols for dealing with students suspected of being at suicide risk and students who make attempts on or off school property, as well as strategies for assisting the school community in the event of a death by suicide.

Where does your school stand in the comprehensiveness of your policy development? The CD-ROM provides a readiness survey that makes it easy to assess how your school currently measures up and where you might need to fill in the blanks. Also provided is a sample policy that covers the essential components around which comprehensive protocols can be structured.

The second level of the competent school community is *prevention.* The essentials of prevention, addressed in *Lifelines: A Suicide Prevention Program,* include several components. Prevention begins with providing youth suicide awareness training for all faculty and school staff. The comprehensiveness of this approach ensures that everyone who comes in contact with students—from classroom faculty to bus drivers to cafeteria staff—understands the importance of their limited but critical role: to identify students who might be at risk for suicide and refer them to the appropriate school resources for assessment. Parents are also recognized as a key piece of the prevention equation, with specific materials designed to increase their awareness about the realities of youth suicide and to prepare them to be advocates for their children in the event they need professional mental health assistance. Finally, students are integrated into prevention by helping them to recognize signs of potential risk in themselves and others and to identify trusted adults to whom they can turn for assistance.

*Intervention,* which is the subject of this manual, recognizes that after potentially at-risk youth are identified, the next step involves referral to school resource staff for initial assessment. Again, in the context of the limited responsibility of the school, the format of this assessment, which is based on clinical interviewing principles, is clearly structured to focus on information that clarifies the school's reasons for concern about the student. It outlines what additional information should be gathered to facilitate a referral to community resources and reviews the necessary documentation to protect the school from liability issues.

The final part of the model, responding in the aftermath of a death within the school community, is covered in *Lifelines Postvention: Responding to Suicide and Other Traumatic Death.* Although *Postvention* may be the least frequently used

**1-1**

**1-2**

*Lifelines* component, it is nonetheless an intrinsic part of a proactive, competent school community that takes its commitment to the safety of its students seriously.

## AS AN ADMINISTRATOR, WHAT ARE THE KEY ASPECTS OF INTERVENTION TO WHICH I NEED TO PAY ATTENTION?

Although many schools handle referral arrangements with local mental health providers in informal ways, there has been increasing recognition of the value of drafting more formalized memorandums that clarify what a school can expect from these community resources. The agreements usually reference the ways in which the agency or provider will respond to requests from the school for risk assessments, clarify the information that will be shared with the school to facilitate the provision of school-based support to an at-risk student who is in treatment, and address how the agency or provider will assist the school in dealing with crises. These types of agreements can be especially helpful when the school is requesting an emergency assessment for imminent suicide risk. This kind of evaluation generally takes place in a crisis center or emergency room. Having established and formalized relationships with these types of referral sources in advance of a crisis can be very helpful in streamlining the process at a point when time may be critical.

These formalized memorandums are not necessary with every provider to whom the school makes referrals. For example, most private mental health practitioners will have their own "release of information" documents which specify the information they've received permission from the parents or guardians to share with the school. When referrals are made to mental health providers, it may be helpful to specifically inform parents that these forms are available and must be signed by them to allow the therapist to communicate limited but essential information to the school so the school can help support their child's mental health needs. Another aspect of record keeping that should concern a school administrator is the form that documents staff contact with a student's parents and subsequent referral recommendations. It can be very important to document that a school has been diligent in turning over its responsibility for the safety of an at-risk student to his or her parents and in requiring follow-up with an off-campus mental health professional. A sample form for documentation of parental/guardian follow-up is located on the CD-ROM.

**1-3**

An administrative issue that frequently challenges school officials when making emergency referrals to crisis services is asking for written documentation that the student is no longer at risk for suicide as a condition of the student's return to school. Although mental health resources are usually able to determine a student's current level of suicide risk and recommend appropriate treatment protocols, they are not able to predict definitively when the risk for suicide has abated.

The unfortunate reality, confirmed by the Youth Risk Behavior Survey conducted annually in schools across the country, is that as many as 13 percent of high school students have considered suicide as an option in the preceding academic year. There will always be students who are at risk for suicide in our schools. That's why it's so important to have a trained faculty and staff who can recognize signs of escalating risk and make referrals for additional assessment. That's also why it's critical to have collaborative relationships with local mental health resources that can provide guidance about the ways in which the school community can support potentially suicidal students.

## WHAT ABOUT THOSE CONFIDENTIALITY CONSTRAINTS IN HIPAA AND FERPA?

First let's talk about HIPAA, which stands for the Health Insurance Portability and Accountability Act, a 1996 federal statute. Although the act actually covers many topics unrelated to privacy, the privacy aspect is what we'll look at in relationship to schools. Covered entities under HIPAA are

- health care clearinghouses

- health plans

- health care providers

A simple rule of thumb is that any provider who bills an insurance company or health plan is a covered entity under HIPAA. Some school districts fit the definition of a "covered entity" under HIPAA because they conduct electronic transactions for payment as Medicaid providers in the School Health and Related Services (SHARS) program. Most school districts, however, do not fit the definition of a "covered entity." To make sure, districts should consult with their legal advisors to determine whether HIPAA applies to them.

Even if a school is covered by HIPAA, however, the HIPAA Privacy Rule authorizes a health care provider to disclose an individual's danger to self or others, without the individual's consent, to another health care provider for that provider's treatment of the individual. What does this mean in a school when there is a student who may be at risk for suicide? Translated into plain English, this means one counselor can share information about a student's suicide risk with another member of the school's resource staff. This can be important to communicate with your resource staff who may misinterpret either HIPAA or the confidentiality protections of their professions to mean that they cannot share what they have been told in the privacy of a counseling session. When there is a question about a person's danger to self or others, confidentiality provisions *do not apply*.

Does this mean a school resource person can tell a teacher about a student's risk for suicide? Yes. Appropriate information needs to be disclosed; however, teachers do not need to know specific diagnoses. Teachers can be told what types of symptoms to look for and what should be done in the event that those symptoms appear. This does not mean that the entire staff need to know about a student's mental health problems. Only the minimum necessary information should be disclosed, and only to those with a justifiable need to know.

Now let's look at FERPA, the Family Educational Rights and Privacy Act of 1974. FERPA had two original goals:

1. To give parents access to the educational records of their children

2. To limit the transferability of records without consent

Despite ambiguities in the original law, it is very clear that nonconsensual disclosures of educational record information in response to an emergency are exempt from the consent requirement (James 1997). It's also important to note that FERPA *does not apply* to shared verbal communication. The need for educators to share and receive information about students potentially at risk for suicide is hard to overstate. As Bernard James, J.D., of the National School Safety Center, eloquently puts it: "Educators' decisions about the needs of a student are based on the quality of the information available to them" (James 1997, 461).

## WHAT IS THE BOTTOM LINE?

When a student is potentially at risk for suicide, there is no confidentiality. The importance of saving a life overrides any expectation of privacy.

## LET'S REVIEW

As an administrator, you must advocate for the policies and procedures that will help your school provide students with a safe learning environment. Making sure your board has approved policies to address the needs of students at risk for suicide is the essential foundation on which all suicide prevention activities must be based. With policies in place, you can begin to establish written protocols that codify the ways in which your school will address the needs of this vulnerable segment of your school's population. A key aspect will be making sure that your resource staff members are prepared to intervene when an at-risk student is identified. The following chapters will walk the reader through the steps of this process. They will highlight key aspects and provide suggestions for the practical application of theory to the realities of today's students and their families.

## IN YOUR
# Experience...

- When was the last time you reviewed your school's policies for at-risk students? Is there anything that needs to be updated?

- Are teachers, staff, and administration aware of the exceptions to FERPA when suicide risk is a possibility?

- Have you had experiences with referring students for outside assessment that worked well? Didn't work at all? What can you learn from these experiences to help you modify your procedures and protocols?

## RESOURCES

Bergren, M. D. "HIPAA Hoopla: Privacy and Security of Identifiable Health Information," *Journal of School Nursing* 17, no. 6 (2001): 336–40.

Health, Mental Health, and Safety Guidelines for Schools: Protection of Student and Staff Confidentiality. See www.nationalguidelines.org/guideline .cfm?guideNum=0-03.

"HIPPA" and "FERPA" Questions & Answers for Schools & Day Cares. See www.dphhs.mt.gov/PHSD/Immunization/documents/HIPPA.doc.

National Association of School Nurses. HIPAA and FERPA information. See www.nasn.org.

National School Boards Association. See www.nsba.org.

National Task Force on Confidential Student Health Information. *Guidelines for Protecting Confidential Student Health Information.* Kent, OH: American School Health Association, 2000.

Youth Risk Behavior Survey. See www.cdc.gov/violenceprevention/pub/youth _suicide.html.

## HANDOUTS

1-1: Readiness Survey

1-2: Suicide Prevention, Intervention, and Postvention Policy and Procedure Guidelines

1-3: Documentation of Parental/Guardian Follow-Up

# Chapter 2

# How Intervention Begins: The Intersection of Values, Knowledge, and Empathy

*"I never thought much about the effect of my personal experiences with suicide on my assessment of risk in students. They never seemed connected until the first time a truly suicidal girl sat across from me and all I could see was my sister Chandra's face. She had taken her life fifteen years previously, and I just assumed I had put her death behind me and it was in the past. How wrong could I be! I was so preoccupied with reliving Chandra's death that I had to struggle to pay attention to this young student's story."*

—SCHOOL COUNSELOR

Although most of us have an intellectual understanding about the ways in which personal beliefs, values, and history shape our experiences, this awareness is usually below our consciousness. We don't often find ourselves cognizant of the fact that our response to a current situation is affected by a multitude of factors that can affect our competence, our sensitivity, and even our decision making. We may think we're being open, nonjudgmental, and impartial, but our perceptions of our own usefulness may be clouded by personal biases and prejudices that can compromise our ability to be effective counselors.

Suicide in particular is one of those life experiences that touches people in deeply emotional ways. This chapter will explore suicide from a historical context to provide an understanding of the stigma that has been a companion to suicide from earliest times. It will highlight the shift in perspective from the view of suicide as a moral or religious failing to the symptom of a mental disorder to help frame suicide in current clinical knowledge and perspective. It will also provide some brief exercises to assist in clarifying personal values about suicide and to facilitate increased understanding of the youthful suicidal mind. This introspection will form the foundation for the development of the empathic skills that are essential to competent intervention with at-risk students and their families.

Finally, this chapter will provide a mental health knowledge base about suicide to guide your interventions.

By the end of this chapter, you will be able to

- understand the ways in which suicide has been surrounded by negative perceptions and stigma

- identify your personal values about suicide

- define the characteristics of suicide and understand how they relate to at-risk students

## WHAT IS THE HISTORICAL PERSPECTIVE OF SUICIDE?

A documented historical perspective of suicide dates to ancient times and reflects the fact that society's views of suicide have been inconsistent. As far back as 500 BC in ancient Greece, suicide was considered a disgraceful act. Life was considered a gift bestowed by the gods, and life and death were subject to the will of the gods. Taking one's own life was seen as rebellion against the gods. In *Laws*, Plato stated that a person who has committed suicide should be buried with no honors in a lonely place where no monuments could be raised on the grave. Nevertheless, he was also convinced that there would be exceptions to the rule. Suicide was acceptable, he wrote, for persons who suffered from horrible ailments, intolerable poverty, or profound grief and need. In Plato's time, the hand used for the act of suicide was cut off and buried far away from other burial sites, and the body was then burned outside the town.

History appears to tell us that suicide was a rare occurrence among Jews. As in ancient Greece, the Old Testament regarded life as sacred, and suicide was considered wrong and unworthy by Jewish law. Those who completed suicide were denied burial according to the common rites. However, exceptions were again made, primarily if suicide would help avoid disgrace through captivity or torture. Christian beliefs at first supported suicide with the belief that "self-chosen death" was something to which the most genuinely pious would aspire. During the early years of Christianity, the number of suicides increased because many people wished to come closer to God and Christ and live with them forever. This increase in suicides was probably also influenced by a certain pessimism concerning life's prospects that was prevalent at the time. Life after death was substantially more important than life on earth, and there was a corresponding yearning for the values of eternity. However, after a sudden onslaught of Christian martyrs and mass suicides, the Judeo-Christian culture began to condemn and stigmatize both eulogies and public mourning for those who died by their own hand. Fast-forward to the Middle Ages, when the social stigma of suicide became even more pronounced. People who died by suicide not only were forbidden a proper burial but their bodies were also disgraced (for example, dragged through the streets or thrown outside for animals to consume). In England, it was against the law to commit suicide, as it was considered self-murder. Any property of the person who committed suicide had to be forfeited to the king. Consequently, families attempted to hide suicides from the authorities. Anyone who had attempted suicide was arrested, publicly shamed, and sentenced to death.

In the fourteenth through sixteenth centuries, during the Renaissance and Reformation, thoughts and attitudes toward suicide became a topic of social interest, particularly among literary and academic circles. Writers such as Shakespeare wrote about characters who died by suicide, perhaps attempting to remind society that, despite the stigma, suicide was an inescapable fact of life. The French philosophers Montesquieu and Voltaire argued in defense of an individual's right to choose suicide.

In the seventeenth and eighteenth centuries, most philosophers condemned suicide, and some writers recognized a connection between suicide and severe mental disturbances. In *The Anatomy of Melancholy*, Robert Burton provided the first "modern" interpretation of suicide, suggesting specifically that suicide can represent an expression of severe depression (melancholy). Even in legal circles, penalties for suicide were less often enforced, as judges realized that sentencing a corpse was irrational, and that the same person, technically, could not be considered both murderer and victim.

With the development of sociology in the nineteenth century, suicide finally became the subject of academic inquiry and study. In his 1897 book *Le Suicide*, Emile Durkheim argued that suicide was not just an individual choice, but that society at large acted as a contributing factor. Durkheim laid the foundations for both sociology and the study of suicide, called suicidology, through his writings, which changed society's views of suicide. Experts in the field have observed that one of the reasons suicide is less stigmatized today is because of Durkheim's understanding that outside pressures, or societal stressors, can contribute to suicidal behavior.

Countries slowly began to abolish laws that made suicide a crime. A significant development occurred in 1983, when the Roman Catholic Church reversed the canon law that prohibited funeral rites and burial in church cemeteries for those who had died by suicide. Unfortunately, the result of this has been paradoxical. While one of the intentions of removing the stigma surrounding suicide was to encourage help seeking and mental health treatment, the prohibition of suicide in religion can serve as a significant protective factor in some cultures.

*"When I was fourteen, I thought about suicide, but knew I would go to hell and I couldn't bear that thought. As I got older, I realized God would forgive me if I took my life. So I made a very serious attempt."*

*—JOANNE, ITALIAN CATHOLIC*

## HOW DOES HISTORY INFORM OUR CURRENT VIEWS OF SUICIDE?

In the United States, attitudes toward suicide historically mirrored the more repressive positions of European countries. A sign of a dramatic and significant change, however, came in 1999 when Surgeon General David Satcher unveiled a blueprint to prevent suicide in the United States. The document, entitled *The Surgeon General's Call to Action to Prevent Suicide,* outlines more than a dozen steps that can be taken by individuals, communities, organizations, and policy makers. Each state is now required to put a plan in place to address suicide prevention. These plans can be found on the website of the Suicide Prevention Resource Center (www.sprc.org).

Unfortunately, despite these national efforts to provide accurate information and education about suicide, the topic of suicide is often still surrounded by negative stereotypes, stigma, and shame. This leads to the lack of identification of risk, and ultimately causes people to not seek help.

*"I am a social worker by training, and when my son died by suicide I was haunted by the fact that I should have known better—I should have recognized the warning signs. I kept to myself for a long time after his death, to deal with my grief and shame. One of the first times I went out in public was to a soccer game for my younger son. I was watching nervously from the sidelines when another parent came up to me. We chatted a bit about the game and then she said it—she confirmed my*

*worst fears. 'Wow, if suicide could happen to you,' she said, 'with all your training, I guess it could happen to any of us.' It took me a moment to catch my breath, but when I did, I told her that, yes, she was right— suicide can happen in any family and I hoped she could learn from my experience to be better prepared."*

—MOTHER OF SUICIDE VICTIM

The good news is that more people, like the woman in the quotation, are overcoming their shame and finding their voices to encourage suicide awareness and to support prevention activities. One of the first steps in suicide prevention is understanding that suicide *can* and *does* happen in any family. The next step is understanding that suicide isn't caused by moral weakness—it usually reflects a mental illness that can be treated.

## WHAT STEPS CAN I TAKE TO BE BETTER PREPARED TO INTERVENE WITH A POTENTIALLY SUICIDAL STUDENT?

The place to start is with yourself. Have an internal dialogue that is thoughtful, honest, and humble to examine your attitudes, values, experiences, and knowledge about suicide.

*"I have an advanced degree in counseling, and I just assumed my graduate training had prepared me to assess a student for suicide risk. But when I heard myself say to a student who had been referred to me for possible suicide risk, 'You don't really want to kill yourself, do you?' I knew I was in trouble!"*

—STUDENT ASSISTANCE COUNSELOR

How do you begin to assess your own values and attitudes about suicide? A simple awareness exercise can help clarify your personal perceptions about suicide and the suicidal mind.

Read through the Suicide Awareness Questionnaire on the next page, and answer each question as honestly as you can. A reproducible copy of this questionnaire is located on the CD-ROM. Remember, your responses reflect personal and private values that are neither right nor wrong—they simply *are*. They are also personal—you do not have to share them with anyone else!

2-1

# Suicide Awareness Questionnaire

1. When I hear the word "suicide," the following words come to my mind:

    a. _____    b. _____

    c. _____    d. _____

    e. _____

2. I think the most positive thing about suicide is: _____

    _____

3. I think the most negative thing about suicide is: _____

    _____

4. What I can understand about suicide is: _____

    _____

5. What I can't understand about suicide is: _____

    _____

6. What would help me better understand suicide is: _____

    _____

7. If you have had either a personal or a professional experience with suicide, take a few minutes to think about the ways in which you were affected by it. The following questions may help you structure your thinking:

    a. How long ago did you have this experience? _____

    b. What was your relationship to the person who attempted or completed suicide?

    _____

    c. Can you remember your initial reaction? _____

    _____

    d. How did others around you respond? _____

    _____

    e. Were your or others' reactions to the death or attempt colored by stigma?

    _____

    f. What was the most difficult or challenging aspect of this experience for you?

    _____

    _____

8. On the following scale, rate your degree of comfort in completing an assessment of a suicidal student:

    _____ Very comfortable       _____ Comfortable       _____ Very uncomfortable

What do your answers on the questionnaire tell you? If you responded thoughtfully, you should get an accurate picture of the intangibles you bring to your interactions with potentially suicidal students. In particular, your answer to question 6 (What would help me better understand suicide?) can point you to additional information that might enhance either your skills or your level of comfort, reflected in question 8.

On the other hand, your responses might alert you to uncomfortable feelings and perceptions that could make it difficult for you to remain nonjudgmental and objective when discussing suicide with a student. Give yourself permission to acknowledge this reaction and see if this personal assessment changes as you read this manual. Many people find that increased knowledge and information about suicide does increase their comfort in approaching the topic with students and their parents/guardians. If it does not, you need to continue to explore information about suicide as well as identify other resources or people within your school to whom you can turn for a more objective consultation.

*"I really couldn't put it into words, but I just started to feel like I couldn't face another day. My house hasn't been the same since my brother died and I've just let everything slide—my grades, my soccer, my girlfriend—it's all in the tank. Actually, I've been thinking about suicide for a while, but when I got into that fender bender with my mom's car, that was it. I was done."*

—SENIOR BOY

## I CAN'T CONCEIVE HOW SOMEONE COULD EVEN THINK ABOUT SUICIDE. WHAT CAN HELP ME UNDERSTAND?

While personal experiences with suicide can certainly affect our reactions to current situations, they may not help us better understand the mind-set of someone who is contemplating suicide. That's when a clear, simple definition of suicide and an explanation of its characteristics may be helpful:

> *Suicide is an attempt to solve a problem of intense emotional pain with impaired problem-solving skills (Kalafat and Underwood 1989, 29).*

There are many ways to think about suicide, but this definition, which frames suicide in a behavioral context, minimizes both judgment and personal interpretation. It reminds us that suicide is a response to something emotionally painful that's going on in a person's life and that the person's response—suicide—results from an impaired ability to cope. This impairment may result from a variety of risk factors.

Edwin Shneidman (1985), one of the first mental health practitioners to study suicide, outlined some basic characteristics of suicide that may help in understanding it. Here is a version of what he had to say.

### 1. Suicide Is Viewed as an Alternative to a Seemingly Unsolvable Problem.

Viewing suicide as an alternative to a problem has several important implications. For one, just as a teen may get a temporary high from a drug, he or she may obtain temporary relief, attention, support, or even popularity after a suicide attempt. Although these "positive" effects do distract temporarily from the problem itself, they are generally short-lived, especially if the basic problems that underlie the attempt aren't addressed. In fact, these initial problems, which prompted the attempt, are usually exacerbated by the stigma that eventually surrounds any suicide attempt.

A second implication of viewing suicide as an alternative is that suicide can then be understood less as a wish to die than as a wish to escape the intense emotional pain generated by what appears to be an inescapable situation. The most relevant question to ask a suicidal teen to clarify the suicidal motivation is "What's going on in your life right now that has you feeling that death is the only answer?" This can begin to frame the discussion about the problem that needs to be solved, rather than the hopeless and helpless feelings that have led to the thought that suicide is an acceptable way out.

When talking about this, however, be careful not to offer the familiar cliché "Suicide is a permanent solution to a temporary problem." Few people really stop to internalize the meaning of clichés, which are dismissive and impersonal. And because so many people have heard the suicide cliché before, few people really

## Characteristics of Suicide

1. Suicide is viewed as an alternative to a seemingly unsolvable problem.
2. Crisis thinking impairs problem solving.
3. A suicidal person is often ambivalent.
4. The choice of suicide has an irrational component.
5. Suicide is a form of communication.

listen to it! With adolescents in particular, the idea that suicide is an alternative for solving a problem provides a very clear frame for questions in the assessment interview. Inexperienced clinicians often make the mistake of asking suicidal people why they want to die and are chagrined to get the answer, "Because I don't want to live." This often is a conversation-stopper. Asking the question, "What do you think happens after you die?" may also result in less than helpful information. Sometimes the meaning of death is to reunite with a loved one, but most youth provide a personal account of a hereafter that includes all the good things about life on earth, devoid of all the problems. Where does this question get you? First of all, it's hard to disagree with someone's expectations of life after death. But more importantly, this type of question doesn't give you any insight into what's provoking the student into thoughts of suicide.

*"When I asked Hector what he thought happened to people after they died, he painted this amazing picture of a heaven filled with soccer fields and parties. 'It will be an eternal good time,' the fourteen-year-old told me. When I tried to point out that I wasn't so sure that heaven was like that, he got really angry. 'You're not God!' he yelled. 'What makes you think you know so much?' Needless to say, the interview went downhill from there."*

*—SCHOOL COUNSELOR*

While Hector's story provides a rather dramatic example of a counselor questioning a student's preconceptions about heaven, it also illustrates the box a counselor can get into when trying to point out the uncertainties about what happens to us when we die. Focusing on a topic that is so personal can also derail the purpose of the interview. Hector makes a valid point—how does the counselor know that he's wrong about what heaven is like? The more relevant question is "What's going on in Hector's life that makes heaven seem like a better place to be?" This discussion puts the assessment process on track and provides a relevant, concrete focus for the counselor's questions rather than setting up a potentially confrontational and contentious atmosphere about the meaning of the hereafter that is likely to go nowhere.

## 2. Crisis Thinking Impairs Problem Solving.

Consider a crisis as any situation in which we feel our skills do not meet the demands the environment is placing on us. If you think about it, no matter how diverse our range of coping skills might be, we will all encounter certain situations for which no backlog of experience seems totally sufficient. Looking at it from this perspective, crises are normal occurrences in the course of everyone's lives. Unfortunately, our reactions sometimes suggest we've never been through a crisis before, as our thinking in a crisis is usually emotional, extreme, limited, and not conducive to effective problem solving.

Perhaps the best way to understand crisis thinking is through the following short exercise.

> *Think of the last time you were in a crisis situation—a time when you felt overwhelmed by what was going on around you. It can be a big crisis or a little one. The scope or the situation itself doesn't matter. Once you have pictured the crisis situation, think about your initial response. How did you feel, physically and emotionally? What did you think? While the thinking of some people gets clearer and more focused in a personal crisis, for most of us the opposite is true. We become emotional, frightened, paralyzed—like a deer in the headlights, as the saying goes—and our bodies respond in kind. Our heart rate increases, our palms may sweat, we may feel nauseated, and our thinking may narrow or constrict to the point that it's hard to formulate alternatives to what created the crisis in the first place. In fact, we may not be able to think of even one solution for solving it.*

Recall what helped you get through the crisis you were just thinking about. Your coping strategies probably included one or more of the following:

- taking a deep breath and trying to relax
- thinking about something else until you feel calmer
- exercising to clear your head
- praying
- talking to a friend

The most universal response tends to be the last one: talking to a friend. But usually the friend we choose is not just any friend. The friends we turn to in crisis seem to have certain characteristics that set them apart from the other members of our support system.

Think again about your personal crisis. If you were going to call a friend to help you get through it, which one of your friends would that be? What characteristics of that person would lead you to choose him or her instead of somebody else? Most likely these would include

- available

- nonjudgmental

- trustworthy—wouldn't tell others about my situation

- understanding

- good listener

Not surprisingly, "good listeners" tend to have these traits in common: they listen patiently, don't interrupt or tell us they've heard the same story before, don't dismiss or diminish our concerns, and don't give unsolicited advice or try to solve the problem for us. These friends don't tell us that we'll get over it or that our feelings are stupid. They acknowledge our concerns and usually ask what they can do to help. In other words, they don't make us feel more out of control than we probably already feel. And by simply listening, they allow us to express our feelings, get a bit of perspective, and figure out what to do on our own. It's not a surprise that these are the skills of telephone crisis hotline volunteers—they have the ability to listen patiently without judgment until the caller has had the chance to express the distressing feelings that have created a problem-solving crisis.

When you're addressing a crisis with a student, these same skills apply. As you know, it often doesn't take much to trigger a crisis, especially in a youngster without the life experience to realize the normality of crises or the fact that they usually do resolve. For a fifth grader, for example, the combination of having a poor night's sleep, losing a fight to his older sister, and being "forced" by his mom to eat breakfast before he leaves for school can make the ground ripe for a crisis in school when he realizes he has forgotten his homework. His cries of "I want to die" can be a reflection of his feeling tired and overwhelmed.

I would choose _____ to talk to if I were in

a crisis situation because_____

_____

_____

_____

With another student, however, the crisis, even by adult reckoning, may be more serious. Students may present with family turmoil or a serious illness—the range of terrible things that can happen in the lives of children is impossible to catalogue. Again, the same good listening skills apply even though the solution may be harder to achieve. Your major goal is to be that impartial person who can hear whatever concerns a student expresses with the same degree of patience, empathy, and interest. Crisis intervention literature tells us that being able to talk through the feelings of crisis with someone who listens is an effective way to reduce their intensity.

Some people epitomize calm, cool, and collected problem solving, even in a crisis. If you are one of these people, you might find it hard to be empathic to students who respond to crises in more emotional ways. This awareness of your own crisis response should lead you to be patient and ask more questions to try to understand the student's perspective.

### 3. A Suicidal Person Is Often Ambivalent.

*Ambivalent* means that a person is feeling two things at the same time. In relation to suicide, there is a part of the person that wants to die and a part that wants to live. When talking with a suicidal student, we must acknowledge both of these components. While we align with and undeniably support the side that wants to live, this can't be done by ignoring or dismissing the side that wants to die. If you think about times in your life when you've had a strong feeling and someone close to you ignored it or told you that you didn't really feel that way, you know that this type of response only makes you feel misunderstood and unsupported. It shuts down communication for good. Acknowledging that a part of the student really wants to die and letting him or her talk about it may be scary, but it will communicate to the student that you are really listening to what he or she is saying. It also shows that you can listen to distressing feelings without getting distressed yourself. In clinical terms, this is defined as being able to "hold" painful emotions. Ignoring or discounting the student's disturbing feelings only raises his or her anxiety and increases the feelings of isolation that are so prevalent in people who are feeling suicidal.

By listening to and acknowledging the ambivalence, you are not supporting the student's wish to die. You are simply acknowledging both sets of feelings! Your ultimate message to the student should be something like this:

> "While I hear you telling me that sometimes you feel so hopeless
> about your future that you want to die, you're also here talking
> with me right now. This is the first step in figuring out another way

to handle this situation so you don't have to die. That's the part of you that I want to work with. Because I think if we put our heads together, we can figure this out."

In an intervention like this, you are also giving the student some of your hope that there is another solution to the problem. When you remember that hopelessness is one of the feelings that characterize suicidal people, you can understand how important this lending of hope can be.

## 4. The Choice of Suicide Has an Irrational Component.

Students who are suicidal are often unaware of the consequences of suicide that are obvious to the rest of the world. For example, they are usually not thinking about the impact of their death on others, or they hold a perception that they will somehow still be present to see how others react to their death. While this irrationality reflects how trapped and helpless the student feels, it can seem impossible to get the student to see another perspective.

*"Bryan insisted that his recent behavior [being suspended for drug use] was so scandalous that his family could never forgive him, despite the fact that his parents had already gotten him an appointment with a drug counselor. He felt he had set such a bad example for his little brother, Seth, that he had no choice but to kill himself. Everyone would be happier this way. Trying to get him to understand that his death would only create more heartache was pointless—he just couldn't wrap his brain around that."*

*—SCHOOL PSYCHOLOGIST*

With a student like Bryan, it is usually more helpful to talk rationally about the reasons he may have for living rather than try to address the irrationality of his thoughts about dying.

*"When I asked Bryan to think about what reasons he might have for living, he seemed taken back. After thinking about it for a while, he reluctantly admitted that he had promised to teach Seth to ride a bike and if he took his own life, there would be nobody to do it."*

### 5. Suicide Is a Form of Communication.

For people who are suicidal, normal communication has usually broken down. The suicide attempt may be their way of sending a message or reacting to the isolation they feel because their communication skills are ineffective. The question that addresses this breakdown can be phrased in the following way: "Who do you want to send a message to and what do you want that message to be?" With students, there is often a message to be delivered to parents like the following:

- "I'm sorry I've caused you so much trouble."
- "I can't live up to what you expect from me."
- "I've tried everything else and nothing works."
- "I told you I needed help."

Having this information gives you another topic to pursue in your assessment: "How can I help you talk to your parents to help them better understand what you're going through right now?"

*"Timothy, a ten-year-old boy who had talked openly with the school nurse about hanging himself, didn't hesitate a second when I asked him who he wanted to send a message to with his suicide. 'My mom and dad,' he said. 'They never think I'm serious when I tell them I'm having problems in school and I never want to go to school again. I hate it. They just say too bad, I have to go. If I die, they can't make me go back to school ever again.'"*

—STUDENT ASSISTANCE COUNSELOR

Timothy illustrates the irrationality contained in suicidal thinking as well as the frustrated attempts at communication. With the counselor as his advocate, Timothy was able to communicate his distress in a nondestructive way that allowed his parents to acknowledge his problems and get him some help.

## LET'S REVIEW

The act of suicide has been colored with personal and societal perceptions since earliest times. Unfortunately, most of those perceptions—and the subsequent assumptions about the person who would think about taking his or her own life— have been negative and critical, which has often compromised and complicated the process of seeking help for suicidality. Understanding suicide from a more objective, behavioral viewpoint and reframing it as an impaired choice in problem solving rather than as a reflection of weakness or character defect is one way to address the stigma that still exists even today.

The next chapter will continue to explore the experience of suicide through the observations and words of youth who have been suicidal.

## IN YOUR
# Experience...

- In your personal or professional experience, what have you found most difficult in dealing with suicide?
- How has your perspective on suicide evolved over the years?
- What personal experiences, if any, have helped you better understand suicide?

## RESOURCES

Jacob Crouch Foundation: The History of Suicide. See www.injacobsmemory.org /history-of-suicide.html.

Retterstol, N. "Suicide in a Cultural History Perspective, Part 1" (originally published in the Norwegian journal *Suicidologi* in 1998). See www.med.uio .no/ipsy/ssff/english/articles/culture/Retterstol1.pdf.

## HANDOUTS

2-1: Suicide Awareness Questionnaire

......................................................................

# Chapter 3

# In Their Own Words: Listen to Youth Speak

*"I am a cutter and I've tried to kill myself, the most recent time being about two weeks ago on Tuesday. I've been bullied since I was seven, yet I didn't realize it until a couple of weeks ago. I have deliberately made myself sick before and starved myself because I'm bigger than most of my friends. In November, I was getting help with a school counselor, but I was missing classes which I just couldn't afford to miss. I haven't gone back because I've been too afraid and my mom doesn't know about my latest suicide attempt. . . . My best friend, Jane, knows about the suicide attempts and we were talking about it one night and I couldn't handle it and went upstairs and locked myself in the bathroom. She followed me and I just sat there feeling nothing. I don't know if I'm just hormonal because I'm fifteen, but this almost-empty feeling has been going on for a while and I just don't know what to do anymore because I've destroyed friendships and don't know what place I am at the moment. Thank you for reading my post."*

—ANONYMOUS POSTING ON THE WEBSITE "TUMBLR"

If you've talked with students who are seriously thinking about dying, you've probably heard remarks similar to those in the website posting. If you are newer to the field, you may not have been faced with the despair and desperation that can permeate a suicidal student's thoughts and feelings. Although the historical and theoretical perspectives of suicide set the stage for a more nuanced appreciation of suicide, this picture still lacks the personal aspects that can help adults truly empathize with how a suicidal youth thinks and feels.

This chapter will add words and personal experiences to the characteristics outlined in chapter 2. These stories and voices of youth from around the globe illustrate the common themes of hopelessness, helplessness, and worthlessness that fill the mind of a suicidal young person.

By the end of this chapter, you will be able to

- understand the ways in which youth experience the five characteristics of suicide

- appreciate the ways in which youth communicate suicidal thoughts and feelings

- consider techniques to increase the empathy you have with suicidal youth

# CHARACTERISTIC 1:

*Suicide Is Viewed as an Alternative to a Seemingly Unsolvable Problem.*

## WHAT PROBLEMS LEAD YOUTH TO THOUGHTS OF SUICIDE?

Most adults have learned that there is often no choice but to confront even massively difficult life problems and figure out how to carry on. We come to expect that there will always be times when life is hard and that, with patience, fortitude, and help from friends, there will be a way to get through. This perspective is based on maturity, age, and an accumulation of life experiences that remind us that tomorrow is another day. A bad week or month or even a bad year can be followed by a time when things fall back into place.

Even those of us who can remember vividly the worst days of our adolescence may have difficulty appreciating what could make a teen feel that life is so bad that death seems like a welcome alternative. It can be hard for us to comprehend how what seem to be minor events and disappointments can cause thoughts of wanting to be dead.

In an effort to answer this question, interviewers asked young people who had survived a suicide attempt questions about the precipitating circumstances. The survivors spoke about many emotions that were attached to a variety of events (Gair and Camilleri 2000). Here are examples of what they told the interviewers:

> "I felt like a real failure. I had just left another school. I was the first person in our family to go to a private school . . . my granddad was

so happy. I had only been there like two weeks . . . but I was really worried about my mum, the stress it would put on her shoulders . . . I took a whole lot of tablets." (Sean, age twenty)

Sean identifies the stress that comes with changing schools and the financial pressure it put on his family. Lena talks about different types of stressors for which she felt responsible. She also speaks about her sense of failure:

"I couldn't go to school without having diarrhea or vomiting . . . and I was putting a lot of stress on my parents. Yeah, what had happened that day, my dad was sick and . . . I thought I was making my dad sick . . . and I thought, 'Yep, I am going to do it.' . . . I went to my best friend and I let it all out and I said I've got to go, you know . . . I felt like such a burden to my parents and I thought I'm no use to anyone, and . . . I'm going to fail high school . . . and I'm not going to get a job. . . . I went home and went to the pantry—my mother is a nurse so we had every drug in the house and I knew which ones to take. I had my mind made up. I took a big glass of water. I took a heap of them and then took the rest." (Lena, age twenty)

Nicci, a thirteen-year-old, described the situation that led up to her suicide attempt this way:

"I hated my teacher, I hated my school, I hated myself. I felt fat and ugly and I had no friends. I couldn't stand the thought of going to high school with these kids and my parents wouldn't let me go to a private school. I'd rather be dead."

Ryan, a ten-year-old, attempted to hang himself after an argument with his parents about walking the dog. Shelley, age sixteen, had just found out she was pregnant. Melanie, thirteen and a childhood cancer survivor, believed that drinking was life-threatening because her liver functioning had been compromised by chemotherapy. Her suicide attempt, drinking a bottle of beer, came after a fight with her older sister.

These few examples point out the extraordinarily wide range of reasons youth provide for wanting to be dead. The fact that we can see that the choice of suicide is an overreaction to their life problems is irrelevant to students. Teens need our empathic understanding of how desperate they must *feel* to even consider suicide as a choice, and our recognition that no matter how resolvable their problems seem to us, they indeed seem insurmountable to them. If we can remember that suicide is not about any one particular problem, but rather is a response to an intense internal or psychic pain caused by the problems from which the youth desperately wants to escape, it will be much easier to engage empathically with a youth's suicidal feelings. These words of an eighteen-year-old girl show the depth of pain that counselors must seek to understand:

> "It really is a morbid thing to ask, but think about it; if somebody that you loved was on their deathbed and going through a *world of pain* being kept alive by machines against their will, and they asked you to pull the plug because they were at peace with dying, *would you let them go?*

> "I know that you're probably thinking that you would only do it if there was no chance of recovery, but what if they didn't want to recover? When I feel suicidal, I don't want to recover!"

*"I met nineteen-year-old Jimmy after he had already made two serious suicide attempts, each of which had resulted in involuntary hospitalization. He had, just barely, graduated from high school the previous year, after experiencing years of school frustration and parental disapproval, especially from his demanding and perfectionist father.*

*"Just prior to his first suicide attempt, Jimmy had been experiencing multiple stressors. He had broken two vertebrae in his back and was unable to work. His steady girlfriend, Sandy, the daughter of his father's employer, had gotten pregnant. Against Jimmy's wishes, she had had an abortion, which the two teens were keeping a secret from their parents. Jimmy was very frightened of his father's anger, especially as his father had warned Jimmy when he had started to date Sandy, 'Don't f\*\*\* this up!' Jimmy started to hear a voice, urging him to kill himself.*

*"Jimmy described himself as 'feeling out of my own control. An invincible force makes the plan and pulls me toward it. I have no feelings.' He described experiencing a 'compulsion to kill myself. I would look for things to do it with, saw myself doing it.' As he told me, 'I used to crave death. Some kids dreamed of college or getting married or buying*

*a house; I dreamed up ways to kill myself. I hated my life. I felt trapped. It was like being in a prison. I never expected to have anything to live for.'"*

—SCHOOL PSYCHOLOGIST

# CHARACTERISTIC 2:

*Crisis Thinking Impairs Problem Solving.*

## WHAT ARE SUICIDAL KIDS THINKING?

In addition to being flooded with negative emotions, suicidal young people experience narrowing of possible problem-solving alternatives, often called "cognitive constriction" or "tunnel thinking." A way to conceptualize this is to picture a funnel. At the top of the funnel, imagine a variety of healthy coping and problem-solving skills, including talking to trusted adults, asking teachers for help, going to counseling—all of the ways teens can try to address the things in their lives that seem overwhelming. Now picture a line that divides the funnel at about midpoint. This line represents the place where healthy problem-solving alternatives switch to those that are not so healthy—social withdrawal, drinking and drugging, aggressiveness—the accumulation of warning signs that suicide risk may be increasing. As teens slide down that funnel, their thinking becomes more and more distorted, and as they look toward the bottom of the funnel, what comes into sharper and sharper focus is the final solution—suicide.

In strikingly similar statements, several survivors of suicide attempts have described this state of mind:

> "When I'm in the tunnel, I shut down. Things look darker and darker, narrower and narrower, and darker. All I see is suicide. I focus on how I would do it, slitting my wrist, taking pills. If I would have been by myself, even with my parents in the house, I would have done it." (Jimmy, age nineteen)

> "It's like walking down a long hallway. It's dark and all the doors on both sides are locked, except for the door at the end of the hallway, and that door says Death." (Senior girl, age sixteen)

In addition to this sense of being in a tunnel or narrow space that seems to be inevitably leading to death, suicidal youth report the other characteristics of crisis thinking that were reviewed in chapter 2. Emotionality, impaired judgment, and the impulsivity of crisis are evident in the following examples:

"I was afraid my parents would ground me for life when they found out I had been drinking at my friend's house. I felt like I had to take the pills—there was no other way out." (Jonah, age twelve)

"I couldn't take it anymore. My father announced he was leaving my mother and I would be stuck living with her. She screamed at him and I screamed back and it seemed like it went on for hours, but maybe it was only a few minutes, but I thought I'm done. I'm done. I'd rather be dead than live with that witch." (Sarah, age sixteen)

"This girl with the locker next to me kept pushing me and the next thing I knew her friends were yelling bad names at me and I decided the way to get back at them was to hang myself in the girl's room and it would be their fault." (Lexi, age eleven)

Another theme that seems to characterize suicidal thinking is the feeling of being separated or isolated from the rest of the world. This anonymous blog from a seventeen-year-old girl captures that feeling quite clearly:

"At its worst, I would feel like I was in a glass container with hard, sharp edges. Even when I was in a room with other people, I wasn't really with them—I just couldn't reach out through the glass. If someone tried to get close to me, they would be stabbed by the hard edges of the glass. It was hard for anything to penetrate that container—even voices seemed to reach me in a slow and garbled way and by the time I would think about something to say back, to be part of a conversation, my thoughts were so slow that I felt like I was always at least three sentences behind. So I just stopped talking. The worst thing was that since people could see through the glass, they thought I was there with them, just like I had been before. I was really suffocating, but no one could see."

# CHARACTERISTIC 3:

*A Suicidal Person Is Often Ambivalent.*

## THE KIDS IN THESE EXAMPLES ALL SEEM PRETTY CLEAR ABOUT THEIR WISH TO DIE. HOW ARE THEY AMBIVALENT?

Recognizing ambivalence can sometimes be challenging. What may seem to outsiders like the will to live can sometimes be viewed by the teen as "part of an act" they are putting on for the benefit of those around them. Tara, seventeen, writes in her blog:

> "There's nothing that annoys me more than my parents continuously saying, 'You seem a little better today.' Shut up! You've said that every day for the longest time and I'm no better and no worse. Shut up! Shut up! Shut up! All the things that I do (shower, comment on TV shows we are watching, move from the couch to a bed), it's an act that's all for them, not because I'm feeling better. If it were up to me, I'd just stay in this spot until my heart stopped."

In a later posting, however, she writes:

> "Today I want to recover, but there's some days when I don't."

She admits that she stays alive for her parents and for one friend:

> "Hear me out, okay? Last night, during one of the hardest nights of my depression, I realized that the only circumstance in which I could seriously take my own life is if the people I loved let me, namely, my parents and one friend. If they won't let me die, I have to live."

As we continue to read Tara's later postings, we can see the hints of ambivalence that were obscured in her earlier writings. She also reminds us of how important it is for counselors to acknowledge both sides of the ambivalence—to recognize that there truly *is* a part of the student that wants to die as well as a small part that still wants to live. As you will see in later chapters, as a counselor, you will support and encourage the part of the student's ambivalence that still holds on to the hope that life can be worth living.

## AS AN ADULT, I KNOW THAT EVEN SERIOUS PROBLEMS CAN GET BETTER. HOW DO I HELP A KID MOVE TOWARD THIS PERSPECTIVE?

Precisely because they are so young, suicidal youth don't have this perspective yet, and because they are feeling suicidal, they are not able to learn or believe it in the moment. As counselors, we can "lend" our own hope about the possibility of feeling better, being careful not to minimize how bad the student is feeling at that moment. We can shift the conversation toward problem solving by saying, "You've told me about the things that have you feeling so bad that you're thinking of suicide. When you've been in difficult situations in the past, what are some of the things you've done that have helped?"

# CHARACTERISTIC 4:

*The Choice of Suicide Has an Irrational Component.*

## ISN'T SIMPLY *THINKING* THAT SUICIDE IS A SOLUTION TO A PROBLEM IN LIFE IRRATIONAL? BY DEFINITION, ISN'T ALL SUICIDAL THINKING IRRATIONAL?

Suicide may seem irrational to those of us on the outside looking in. However, to a young person who is thinking about suicide, the consequences of death often seem preferable to living with what seem like insurmountable problems. This is how eighteen-year-old Joanne explains it:

> "I've had an okay life, but I would be so happy to leave it now and there would be no better way to go than with the people I love by my side wishing me peace. Then I could leave and I wouldn't have to suffer anymore and everyone would know that I died happily and that it's better that I'm gone. This is all really morbid, but if you've ever had depression you know how wonderful the thought of not existing anymore is."

While Joanne's description of suicide as a "happy death" that leaves everyone who loves her feeling good may ring true to her, the irrationality of her expectations about the impact of her suicide seem obvious. This type of irrationality is also evident in seventeen-year-old Josh, a senior who made a very serious suicide attempt. He had just returned to school after three months in drug rehabilitation and had seemed so proud of his initial steps in recovery that everyone in the school was stunned when he attempted to take his own life. "My recovery was feeling shaky and I felt I had only one choice," he explained, "to use again or to die. And since I had worked so hard to get straight, I knew I couldn't choose drugs, so I had to die."

## DO SUICIDAL KIDS EVEN UNDERSTAND WHAT DEATH MEANS?

Regardless of age, understanding death would be a cosmic accomplishment! While this question is probably best addressed by theologians and philosophers, a more relevant concern in our understanding of suicidal youth is whether or not they understand the *consequences* of death. Most suicidal kids simply equate being dead with not feeling so bad anymore, not with being gone from this life forever.

In fact, what most youth do lack is an appreciation for the *finality* of death. Because most teens have limited exposure to the death of people with whom they are close, their imaginings of death may be that it is simply a different, changed version of life.

Memory profiles for deceased peers on social networking sites like Facebook are full of quotations about joining each other in heaven to enjoy the eternal version of the activities they did together on earth. Life seems to continue after death, just in a faraway place called heaven.

The following are actual postings on an "In Memory of" site for a seventeen-year-old senior who died by suicide:

- "Hey Bud, can't wait to join you in heaven for a few brews and a soccer game."

- "We'll be together all together 4ever like in mr p's class."

- "U R my hero…wait for me See U soon."

When death doesn't carry the weight of being removed forever from the people and things you love, suicide can simply become another choice introduced into the youth's repertoire of problem-solving skills. The more often it is considered, the less extreme it seems.

*"Once it came into my mind, it never went away. From the moment I decided my life no longer had any value to me, suicide seemed like the easiest solution to everything. It was like the secret I kept in my back pocket—nothing or nobody could hurt me anymore because I had taken that power for myself. Fail a test? Maybe I'll die. Get dumped by a date? Just go to eternal sleep. Fight with my parents? So long forever. The finality of this choice never really occurred to me; I was so caught up in the emptiness and pain that seared my guts from the moment I opened my eyes that the only question I considered was 'How long can I bear to live?' not 'How long will I be dead?'"*

—MOLLIE, AGE EIGHTEEN

# CHARACTERISTIC 5:

*Suicide Is a Form of Communication.*

## WHAT MESSAGES ARE KIDS TRYING TO SEND THROUGH SUICIDE?

Often, the messages contained in suicidal impulses relate back to those unsolvable problems that triggered the suicidal thinking. When asked to whom they wanted to send a message and what they wanted that message to be, consider how some teens responded:

> Tyra (age thirteen): "I wanted those kids at school to know how mean they had been to me."

> Dominick (age twelve): "I knew it would get my mom upset and I was really mad at her."

> TJ (age fifteen): "Message? No f***ing message. It's pretty clear it was an act of defiance to all the fools who have been messin' with me."

> Astrid (age seventeen): "It's a message to everyone that I can't do it anymore. I can't put up with the demands, the pressure, the expectations, the disappointments—the list goes on and on. Nobody has been listening to what I've been saying so maybe they'll listen to this. And if they don't, well, it's still the same thing, isn't it? Who cares?"

**3-1**

The document Understanding the Mind of a Suicidal Teen located on the CD-ROM provides some additional insight into the thoughts and feelings of one suicidal teen through a series of poems written over the course of several years. They dramatically illustrate the five characteristics of suicide through this struggling teen's voice.

## SPEAKING OF COMMUNICATION, HOW CAN I GET A SUICIDAL KID TO OPEN UP TO ME?

No one type of communication style works with every student. However, if you couple your listening skills with a genuine desire to understand the uniqueness of each student's story, you'll be on the right track to getting a student to open up. Here's how one student explained it to his school psychologist:

> "You would say, 'Just try to describe what it's like up in your head, I really want to try to understand,' and then you would just listen. You were soft-spoken, not intimidating, not telling me I didn't feel like that or that things weren't so bad."

This student reminds us again about one of the basics in counseling, especially with adolescents: to see the world through their young eyes. And while this chapter may have helped in your understanding of the inner life of a suicidal student, it can only begin to open up that door. Because each student is unique and will frame thoughts and feelings about suicide in his or her own unique perspective, it is important to avoid the trap that can be set when you say, "I understand how you feel."

---

## What Youth Say Would Help

- Information about depression
- Knowing there is somewhere to go for help
- A caring listener
- Having friends who understand

---

Colin (age sixteen): The first counselor I saw told me she understood how I felt. Who was she kidding? She had to be like ninety years old—she had no idea what my world was like. The next person they sent me to was some guy who looked kinda dorky, but when he told me he didn't understand what was going on with me but that he wanted to—well, that made me think that maybe this was going to be okay. And it was.

## WHAT ELSE CAN WE LEARN FROM YOUNG PEOPLE WHO HAVE SURVIVED A SUICIDE ATTEMPT?

In interviews with young people who survived a suicide attempt, the youth and young adults identified several strategies they felt could improve intervention services. Several participants mentioned getting more education about depression:

- "I think more education in schools would have helped me, if someone had come along and said what depression is and some of the side effects—if you feel like this, there is somewhere you can go." (Sean, age twenty)

- "One thing that did help is knowing that this [depression] is a disease." (Lena, age twenty)

- "My mum . . . works in a health setting. I think that had a lot to do with me actually asking for help. She gets hold of a lot of material for me. I learned a lot about it [depression], that it's not my fault, I can't deal with it myself . . . that most people can't. It all came flooding back. I asked Mum, 'Take me to a doctor. I need some help.'" (Sean)

Youth also talked about the importance of having a caring, approachable listener:

- ". . . just listen and maybe don't try and pry it out of them, you know, just listen. . . . Maybe get them to talk to a friend and ask if you can be there. Maybe they're more comfortable that way." (Lena)

- "If they were caring and understanding, easy to approach . . . paid attention to what I wanted to say." (Lilly, age twenty-two)

Finally, several participants mentioned that it would have been easier for them to approach a friend or a peer:

- "The thing is they have all these suicide programs, counselors, and what have you. Well, maybe *I* don't know the answer, but they haven't got it at the moment either. They can open a counselor shop on every street corner and I guarantee you not one young person who really and truly wants to kill themselves will walk in there. I mean, you talk to your friends, don't you?" (Tina, age eighteen)

- "The counselor has to be your friend or you aren't going to talk to them." (Mandy, age sixteen)

As we've seen before, the fact that youth often turn to peers or friends first is another reason to create that competent school community in which everyone, including the students, is prepared to recognize and immediately respond to a student in need. While the role of peers may be the first step in the process, the next step is to approach a trusted adult. When this message is clearly delivered to the entire school, there is a greater chance that everyone will join together to create a coordinated safety net to protect at-risk youth.

## LET'S REVIEW

While theory is the way to ground any beginning appreciation of the mind of a suicidal child or teen, unless it's translated into the words and experiences of the kids we're trying to serve, knowledge alone can be useless. This chapter captured the voices of youth who have felt their lives were on the edge. In the language and nuance of their own words, they explain to us, the grown-up outsiders, how they think and feel about wanting to die. Although these examples provide only a microscopic look at kids who struggle with thoughts of suicide each day, they do illuminate our need to ask enough questions to try to understand each at-risk child we encounter. Youth will tell us how to be helpful to them if we ask, and they can be generous in their explanations of what we *don't* understand. We need to be equally generous in our curiosity about the painful world they inhabit and what we can do to help them.

The following chapters will build on both the theory and personal experiences of suicidal youth to create an intervention structure. Read on!

## IN YOUR
# Experience . . .

- What have been your personal challenges in understanding a student's reasons for suicide?
- Can you think of a particular suicidal student for whom you felt a lot of empathy? What was that student's story?
- What are two "take-aways" from this chapter?

## HANDOUTS

3-1: Understanding the Mind of a Suicidal Teen

# Chapter 4

# Identification:
# Who Are the Students Who
# Might Be At Risk?

*"I understand that there are certain lists of so-called risk factors for suicide. But when I read them, they sound like almost every student in the school. Everyone can't be at risk for suicide, or can they?"*

—STUDENT ASSISTANCE COUNSELOR

As this counselor astutely points out, reading lists of youth suicide risk factors can be like reading the attendance roster in a classroom—every student seems to be named in one way or another. And while these risk factors are obviously important to recognize, how can they be utilized in a school setting to discern which students need to be referred to school resource staff for assessment and which students are simply kids muddling through the challenges of adolescence? And what are the "warning signs" that indicate a student might really be on that suicidal edge?

The *Lifelines* model has tried to clarify the differences between the laundry list of risk factors and the more discrete list of warning signs by using the analogy of a traffic signal. Consider the risk factors to be the yellow lights that tell us to slow down and proceed with caution. We need to keep our eyes open and be alert. When the light turns red, however, we need to stop. The red lights, or warning signs, are our signals to call in additional resources and support. You never want to be sitting at a red light by yourself with a potentially suicidal student.

Duplicating this page is illegal. Do not copy this material without written permission from the publisher.

**45**

It's important to remember, however, that each traffic signal also contains a green light, and in our analogy to youth suicide prevention, the green lights stand for protective factors. These are the things that buffer youth from the stresses of adolescence and can protect them from risk factors that seem endemic to growing up. We'll talk about these in more detail in chapter 10.

This chapter will divide the list of risk factors for suicide into specific categories of risk that may be easier to understand. It will also review the warning signs to provide a framework for our interventions in the school with students who appear to be at elevated risk. Because the information in this chapter is based on research, you'll find a lot of statistics and references to data. Over the course of time, you'll want to continue to review the national resources at the Suicide Prevention Resource Center website (www.sprc.org), where you can keep up with current data and evolving research.

By the end of the chapter, you will be able to

- understand the different categories of risk factors for youth suicide

- understand the difference between risk factors and warning signs

- name the signs of elevated risk

- know how to locate nationally recommended programs for prevention and intervention

## WHAT DOES THE PHRASE "RISK FACTOR FOR SUICIDE" ACTUALLY MEAN?

A risk factor for suicidal behavior is a characteristic or situation that has been demonstrated through research to be associated with suicidal behavior for a particular group of people. This risk factor is not necessarily the direct cause of a suicide. Rather, an individual with this particular characteristic or situation is more likely than someone who does not have that risk factor to think about, attempt, or die by suicide.

## WHAT FACTORS PUT KIDS AT RISK FOR SUICIDE?

No one risk factor can definitely identify a youth at risk for attempting or completing suicide. In fact, a variety of factors generally interact and overlap to create differing levels of risk from low through moderate and high. Picture several circles that overlap at a central point of connection. Imagine that each of these circles represents a risk factor domain for suicide. These risk domains include such things as demographic variables, clinical or psychological factors, family factors, stressors, previous attempts, and access to the means to kill one's self.

**Chapter 4**   Identification: Who Are the Students Who Might Be At Risk?

**47**

# Overlap Theory of Suicide

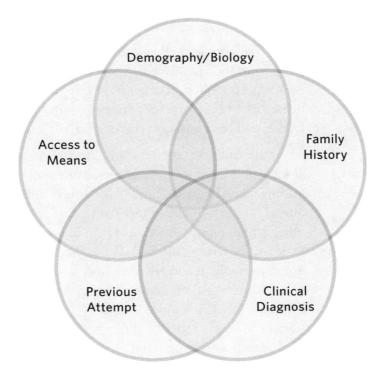

This diagram illustrates that there is never just one cause or risk factor for a suicide; every suicide has multiple variables or is what is called "multidetermined." In reality, these variables exist independently but are pushed into alignment or overlap by what is called a "triggering event." Especially when a suicide receives a lot of media attention, there may be an attempt to identify just one reason or cause for the death, which is often simply the trigger for the death. Sometimes overzealous media want to capitalize on a dramatic aspect of the death (for example, "Teen bullied to death in upper class suburb" or "Pressure drives teen to grizzly suicide"). On other occasions, it is just an attempt to create an understandable reason for the death. We want to believe that being able to explain why the suicide happened will help us avoid the same cause and, therefore, the same result for ourselves and our loved ones.

The good news about suicide being multidetermined, however, is that changing one of the risk variables can often lessen the overall level of risk and provide the opportunity for intervention. Keep this in mind as you read through this section and see whether you can identify risk factors that can be most easily modified or changed.

Lifelines Intervention
. . . . . . . . . . . . . . . . . . . . . . . . . . . . . . . . . . . . . . . . . . . . . . . . . . . . . . . . . . . . . . . . . . . . . . . . . . . . . . . . . . . . . . . . . . . . . . . .

**48**

## HOW DO WE KNOW SO MUCH ABOUT THESE SUICIDE RISK FACTORS?

Our understanding of the most common factors for suicide comes from data in death certificates as well as from "psychological autopsies," studies of youth who have attempted as well as completed suicide. A psychological autopsy uses interviews with individuals who knew the deceased and administrative records (coroner's reports, police reports, etc.) to reconstruct the person's life, thoughts, feelings, behaviors, and experiences prior to death. The information in this chapter on risk factors and warning signs comes from these sources.

Youth from certain demographic groups, for example, have been shown to be at increased risk for suicide. Suicide rates are the highest (and actually the second-leading cause of death) among American Indian and Alaskan Native youth with a rate of 20 per 100,000 compared to approximately 11 deaths per 100,000 among other ethnic groups (CDC, 2010a). Among the major ethnic groups in the United States, Caucasian youth have the highest rate of suicide completions, followed by African American and Hispanic youth. However, over the past few years, the rate of suicide completion among African American youth has substantially increased (Berman, Jobes, and Silverman 2006). Ethnic differences among youth who make suicide attempts reflect a slightly different picture. The rate of suicide attempts has become a growing issue, particularly among African American and Hispanic females. Recently their rates of attempts (11 percent and 10 percent attempts per year, respectively) have bypassed the rates of Caucasian females (6.5 percent) (CDC 2010b). The attempt rates for males are relatively stable across ethnic groups (approximately 5 percent for African American and Hispanic males and approximately 4 percent for Caucasian males).

Age is another demographic variable implicated in suicide risk. While youth ages fifteen to twenty-four experience suicide as the third-leading cause of death nationally, within that age bracket, nineteen-year-old males tend to have the highest rates. It's important to note, however, that the recent spate of suicides in the military have been increasing the rates for the nineteen- to twenty-four-year-old population.

Males and females are at increased risk for different types of suicidal behavior. Males consistently have higher rates of completions than females (11 compared to 2 per 100,000) (CDC 2010a), while females report a higher rate of suicidal thoughts, plans, and attempts (CDC 2010b). The differences in deaths versus attempts are usually attributed to choice of method. Males tend to choose more violent and lethal methods (such as firearms) while females are more likely to use suffocation or poisoning. It's important to point out that when guns are available at home, the risk of both suicide and violence increases (Resnick et al. 1997). This suggests the need for families to be advised to restrict access to guns—or means—if their child

**Chapter 4**  Identification: Who Are the Students Who Might Be At Risk?

**49**

is at risk for suicide. Research suggests that suicide can be decreased if the access to means is reduced or eliminated (Beautrais, Fergusson, and Horwood 2006).

*"After Kevin shot himself, someone asked me if there was any kind of message I wanted to give to the other parents in his school. It didn't take me a minute to think about what it was. Get rid of your guns! It wasn't enough that his father's rifle was dismantled in the garage. Kevin had been hunting with his dad since he was about seven years old and he knew how to put the rifle together. It should have been out of the house! We knew he was depressed and we were taking him for treatment . . . doing all the right things but what turned out to be the most important one—getting rid of the gun."*

*—MOTHER OF SIXTEEN-YEAR-OLD BOY*

While it is important to recognize who may be at risk based on age, gender, or ethnicity, these are simply demographic factors. A variety of other categories of risk factors may also play a role in whether youth try to kill themselves. Risk factors for suicide include psychological disorders, substance abuse, family factors, and adverse life events. Let's look individually at each of these major risk factors.

## A STUDENT HAS BEEN DIAGNOSED WITH DEPRESSION AND IS STILL AT SCHOOL. SHOULD WE BE WORRIED ABOUT THE POSSIBILITY OF SUICIDE?

Depression is one of the psychological or clinical risk factors for suicide attempts and completions, although there are many depressed youth who are not suicidal. It is important, however, to keep your eyes on the students in your school whom you know to be depressed since approximately half of all youth who died by suicide were depressed at the time of their death (Shaffer et al. 1996; CDC 2010b). The good news is that depression is a treatable mental health problem. Significant evidence demonstrates that depression can be alleviated with talk therapies such as cognitive behavioral therapy and interpersonal psychotherapy, with medication, or with a combination of treatments. However, few adolescents actually receive the treatment that is needed. An important way in which the school can intervene is by identifying and referring these youth for proper outside support and treatment.

Most individuals recognize that someone who is depressed may appear to be sad. However, depression in adolescents can be expressed not only as sadness but also as irritability, anger, aggressiveness, or hopelessness. Symptoms such as these have been related to suicide (Gould et al. 1998; Shaffer et al. 1996) although these behaviors may be gender-specific. For example, aggression is a particular risk factor for suicide attempts among boys but not as much for girls (Gould et al. 1998).

The risk of suicide has been shown to increase when a youth is experiencing both depression and another mental health disorder or problem at the same time. In a study of a community sample of adolescents, youth who had depressive and anxiety disorders and those who were depressed and displaying a disruptive behavior disorder were at much greater risk for suicide attempts (Foley et al. 2006).

Your role, of course, is not to provide a mental health diagnosis for any of these problems. That's the job of the community practitioner to whom you make a referral. It can be helpful, however, to simply recognize the complexity of the interrelated emotional issues with which suicidal youth often struggle.

## WHAT IS THE RELATIONSHIP BETWEEN YOUTH SUICIDE AND SUBSTANCE ABUSE?

There is a lot of overlap between the risk factors for suicide and the risk factors for substance abuse. These include poor problem-solving skills, poor social skills, poor coping skills, problematic peer relationships, and family problems. It's especially important to note that *substance abuse is the third most important risk factor for*

### What Is the Choking Game?

Known across the country by many different names (roulette, space monkey, California high, funky chicken, gasp, blackout, flatliner, etc.), the choking game refers to self-strangulation. The flow of blood is cut off to the brain, which results in a feeling of light-headedness or euphoria. Even adolescents who do not drink alcohol or use drugs have used the choking game to feel "high." One study by the U.S. Centers for Disease Control and Prevention (CDC) found sufficient evidence to indicate that since 1995 at least eighty-two youth between the ages of six and nineteen have died in the United States as a result of the game (roughly 1 percent of the deaths attributed to suicide by suffocation in the same age group). Of these youth, 86.6 percent were male, the mean age being 13.3. More than 95 percent of these deaths occurred while the youth was alone; parents of the deceased youth were unaware of the game in 92.9 percent of cases.

**Chapter 4** Identification: Who Are the Students Who Might Be At Risk?

**51**

*youth suicide,* the first and second being a previous suicide attempt and depression (Forman and Kalafat 1998).

Substance abuse plays an important role in the transition from thinking about killing oneself to actually making a suicide attempt. Does the alcohol or drug reduce the inhibitions of depressed youth who are thinking about suicide, which allows them to act? Or does the alcohol or drug increase impulsiveness and aggression, allowing youth to act on their suicidal thoughts? While these questions are important, the answers are unclear. However, it is common for youth who kill themselves to have depression coupled with substance abuse, disruptive behavior disorder, or both (Shaffer et al. 1996). This is another example of a co-occurring disorder. These relationships may vary by gender: girls who demonstrate classic symptoms of depression combined with using substances are more at risk for suicide, and boys who manifest depression through aggressive antisocial behaviors combined with using substances are more at risk for suicide.

## WHAT IF A STUDENT HAS A FAMILY HISTORY OF SUICIDE? CAN SUICIDE "RUN" IN A FAMILY?

Family history *is* important. There is an increasing amount of evidence from research studies on the neurobiology of mental illness that suicide may have some

### The Story of Todd

Todd, an eighteen-year-old boy, attempted suicide after coming home from a graduation party for his ex-girlfriend. She had broken up with him right before prom and had asked another boy to take her. Todd had then asked five other girls, all of whom turned him down. At the party, Todd drank all night and again in the morning. He then drove home and tried to hang himself. Fortunately, his parents found him in time.

Todd later told his counselor that he had tried to hang himself because he had drunk too much and because his ex-girlfriend had let him drive home drunk. "She couldn't have cared about me if she let me drink and drive." He feared he had destroyed any chance for a better social life: "I don't have a good reputation because of the drinking and drugs. Good kids won't hang out with me." Todd also felt hopeless about his future. He had not applied to college, but was planning to attend the local community college, which he negatively regarded as "grade 13."

genetic basis. We also know from social modeling theory that there may be tacit permission in a family touched by suicide for other family members to consider suicide as a problem-solving option. Most of the time, however, you won't be privy to knowledge about a family's history of suicide. What you may know about, however, are families whose functioning is severely compromised by alcoholism or other kinds of addiction, fighting, physical violence, or other stressors that negatively impact a student's functioning. Again, while not all these kids are at risk for suicide, they can benefit from the watchful eye of a caring adult who can serve as a buffer from some of their personal stress.

## ONE OF OUR STUDENTS HAS RETURNED FROM BEING HOSPITALIZED FOR A SUICIDE ATTEMPT. IS HE STILL AT RISK FOR SUICIDE?

The evidence consistently shows that the number one risk factor for suicide is a prior suicide attempt (Brent et al. 1999; Shaffer et al. 1996; Borowsky, Ireland, and Resnick 2001). Many people have tried to understand this phenomenon, and again, questions are raised for which there are not clear answers. Is the risk high because of a learned behavior? Is the risk high because the behavior has been practiced? Is the risk high because, in the future, when things aren't going well, suicide looks like an option? While the answers to these questions may be hard to pinpoint, it's very clear that youth who have a mental health disorder or have made a prior attempt need to be receiving mental health treatment to address the underlying issues and concerns. As long as youth are receiving or have received help for their issues, there is no reason that they cannot practice more adaptive problem solving and continue to succeed in school despite their prior suicidal history. However, school staff members need to keep these students on their radar because if there is a traumatic death in the community or school, these vulnerable youth may need special attention and a "check-in" as part of a postvention school approach to youth suicide. Exposure to the death of another youth, regardless of the cause, or even to the death of someone whom the youth views as a role model, can increase the risk level in vulnerable youth and is actually considered to be another risk factor.

## IS IT TRUE THAT YOUTH FROM DIVORCED FAMILIES ARE AT GREATER RISK FOR SUICIDE?

This is an important question since it reflects a commonly held belief about the negative impact of divorce on children. Family factors can play a role in risk for suicide among adolescents. However, it may not be the divorce that is the actual risk factor. While research has demonstrated that youth who complete suicide are

**Chapter 4**   Identification: Who Are the Students Who Might Be At Risk?

**53**

more likely to come from families that are not intact (Gould et al. 2003), divorce and single parenthood are not considered to be noteworthy risk factors after parental and youth psychological histories are considered. Other factors in the student's family life may be more significant risk factors than the simple fact of parental divorce.

## OUR STUDENTS ARE HIGH-PERFORMING STUDENTS AND UNDER PRESSURE TO DO WELL. DOES THIS INCREASE THEIR RISK FOR SUICIDE?

To the authors' knowledge, there have been no studies examining the effect of everyday pressures and stress on suicide. This being said, there is evidence that certain adverse life events or stressors may be triggers or precipitating events that lead a youth to attempting and completing suicide—a sort of "straw that breaks the camel's back" phenomenon. Many youth may have a multitude of the risk factors for suicide described above and still be functioning well. Then, however, the youth experiences a triggering event, which leads to a downward spiral, a suicide attempt, and potential death.

Precipitating or trigger events for adolescent suicide attempts include interpersonal losses such as a breakup, legal and disciplinary problems, and conflicts at home, in school, or with the law (Gould et al. 1998; Beautrais, Joyce, and Mulder 1997). In a study of suicides in sixteen states, Karch and colleagues (2009) found that approximately a third had an interpersonal problem with an intimate partner and just under a third reported a "crisis" in the two weeks prior to killing themselves (note that these data also included adult deaths). From interviews with Latina adolescents who attempted suicide, a slightly different dynamic on

---

### Risk Factors for Youth Suicide

- Prior attempt
- Mental health problem (for example, depression, anxiety, or a conduct disorder)
- Substance abuse
- Access to means
- Exposure to the death of a peer
- Family history of suicide
- Triggering event

the triggers to suicide attempts emerged. Latina adolescents still reported experiencing a loss. However, the loss resulted from a disruption of the family structure due to divorce, migration, or death, which then led to loneliness and disconnection. Other triggers for the Latina youth included mother-daughter conflict and feeling powerless due to physical or sexual abuse and bullying (which is discussed in chapter 9) (Zayas et al. 2010). Additional categories of special risk addressed in chapter 9 include gifted students, students with learning disabilities, and sexual minority students.

So in summary, you can see that many factors or variables can create potential risk for suicide. Although the factors exist independently, when a youth is in a crisis the factors can come together to create the perfect storm of risk that can increase the odds of a suicide event.

And what risk factors can be changed? The easiest one to modify is one of the most lethal: access to means, especially firearms. Mental disorders such as depression and anxiety can also be changed if the youth can get access to treatment. Substance abuse can also be modified. None of these risk factors can be changed, however, if they're not identified, which is why their recognition is so essential!

## WHAT ARE WARNING SIGNS FOR SUICIDE?

While risk factors can be described as more distant, underlying issues, warning signs can be understood as more immediate indicators of a pending attempt—the red lights on the traffic signal that tell us to stop immediately. Again, even though someone is demonstrating a "warning sign," that does not mean he or she is definitely going to attempt suicide. Just as an understanding of risk factors can lead to identification and reduction of potential sources of risk, our attention to warning signs can assist us in getting a student to appropriate resources in time to avert a suicidal crisis.

The warning signs of suicide that are typically identified by the general public include telling someone of the intent to die, giving away treasured possessions, and leaving a suicide note. Unfortunately, these indicators are rare. Only a third of completed suicides either told someone about their intent or left a suicide note (Karch et al. 2009).

Since we cannot be sure that youth will actually tell someone they are thinking about killing themselves, it's essential that gatekeepers such as teachers, administrators, school nurses, counselors, and other school personnel be aware of other warning signs. In the *Lifelines* model, the mnemonic FACTS organizes the warning signs of suicide. See the sidebar FACTS: The Warning Signs of Suicide on page 55 and the FACTS handout on the CD-ROM.

**4-1**

**Chapter 4** Identification: Who Are the Students Who Might Be At Risk?

**55**

## FACTS: The Warning Signs of Suicide

### Feelings

- Hopelessness: feeling like things are bad now and won't get any better
- Fear of losing control, going crazy, harming himself/herself or others
- Helplessness: a belief that there's nothing that can be done to make life better
- Worthlessness: feeling like an awful person and that people would be better off if he/she were dead
- Hating himself/herself, feeling guilty or ashamed
- Being extremely sad and lonely
- Feeling anxious, worried, or angry all the time

### Actions

- Drug or alcohol abuse
- Talking or writing about death or destruction
- Aggression: getting into fights or having arguments with other people
- Recklessness: doing risky or dangerous things

### Changes

- Personality: behaving like a different person, becoming withdrawn, tired all the time, not caring about anything, or becoming more talkative or outgoing
- Behavior: can't concentrate on school or regular tasks*
- Sleeping pattern: sleeping all the time or not being able to sleep at all, or waking up in the middle of the night or early in the morning and not being able to get back to sleep
- Eating habits: loss of appetite and/or overeating and gaining weight
- Losing interest in friends, hobbies, and appearance or in activities or sports previously enjoyed
- Sudden improvement after a period of being down or withdrawn

*FACTS: The Warning Signs of Suicide continued on next page*

**FACTS: The Warning Signs of Suicide** (continued)

**Threats**

- Statements like "How long does it take to bleed to death?"

- Threats like " I won't be around much longer" or "Don't tell anyone else . . . you won't be my friend if you tell!"

- Plans like giving away favorite things, studying about ways to die, obtaining a weapon or a stash of pills: the risk is very high if a person has a plan and the way to do it.

- Suicide attempts like overdosing, wrist cutting

**Situations**

- Getting into trouble at school, at home, or with the law

- Recent loss through death, divorce, or separation; the breakup of a relationship; losing an opportunity or a dream; losing self-esteem

- Changes in life that feel overwhelming

- Being exposed to suicide or the death of a peer under any circumstances

*One of the essential elements in seeking out possible suicide warning signs is noticing the changes in a student's behavior that signal something is going on that's impacting the student's mood or behaviors. This is a red flag and signals the need for immediate attention.

Specific warning signs often observed by staff in the school include these:

- Teachers may see increased anxiety and/or agitation, lack of focus or concentration, dramatic mood changes, disruptive behavior, withdrawal from friends or academic activities.

- Administrators, especially those in disciplinary positions, may observe more disruptive behavioral issues, such as rage, anger, or recklessness, or engaging in risky activities, seemingly without thinking. There may be reports of alcohol or drug use.

- Counselors and school nurses may see more clinical and physical symptoms, such as tiredness and fatigue, and anxiety symptoms, such as headaches or stomachaches.

Regardless of one's role in the school, however, whenever a warning sign for suicide is identified, that student *must* be referred for more in-depth assessment and screening.

**Chapter 4** Identification: Who Are the Students Who Might Be At Risk?

**57**

## HOW EFFECTIVE ARE PROGRAMS THAT SCREEN STUDENTS FOR SUICIDE RISK?

Screening for suicide risk involves having youth complete a survey about whether they are experiencing any of the risk factors for suicide, such as prior suicide attempt, depression, or substance abuse. After completing the ten- to fifteen-minute screen, youth who indicate they are experiencing the risk factors are then interviewed by a clinical school professional. If it is determined that a youth needs further assessment, the parents are contacted and assisted in finding an appropriate community service.

School-based screening can be used with everyone in the school or with a targeted at-risk population, but it won't, with absolute certainty, identify all youth who may be suicidal. Despite its limitations, however, screening can be a helpful tool. One of the most respected screening programs is the Columbia University TeenScreen program (Shaffer et al. 2004; Scott et al. 2009, 2010).

The TeenScreen program (www.teenscreen.org) is based on the philosophy that it is important to identify youth with untreated depression since depression can lead to school problems, relationship problems, substance abuse, and suicide attempts and completions. The Columbia Suicide Screen (Shaffer et al. 2004)—one measure that the TeenScreen program uses—asks about the main risk factors for suicide, including depression, anxiety, substance abuse, suicidal ideation, and prior suicide attempts. The Columbia Suicide Screen has been shown to effectively identify youth at high risk for suicide as well as youth with other clinical problems (Shaffer et al. 2004; Scott et al. 2010). Furthermore, screening has been shown to be effective in identifying youth at risk for suicide who were currently not identified as a concern by school professionals (Scott et al. 2009).

## HOW DO I GO ABOUT LOCATING PREVENTION PROGRAMS THAT ARE EFFECTIVE IN THE SCHOOL?

Currently, several approaches have been shown to be effective in identifying youth at risk for suicide. The National Registry of Evidence-based Programs and Practices (NREPP, http://nrepp.samhsa.gov), compiled by the Substance Abuse and Mental Health Services Administration (SAMHSA), is a list of mental health programs that have been reviewed and evaluated by a panel of independent reviewers for scientific merit. The programs listed on the NREPP website are identified as "evidence-based" programs, meaning the programs have been evaluated and outcomes have proven the programs' effectiveness. Not all programs that are effective are listed, but the website gives some guidance as to what is available. The Suicide Prevention Resource Center (www.sprc.org) also maintains a list of evidence-based practices, as well as expert consensus statements and a list of other programs that adhere to best-practice standards but have not yet been scientifically validated. All these resources are available online, and you are encouraged to review them regularly to keep up with the latest resources in the field.

## LET'S REVIEW

Suicide is seldom a random event that occurs without warning. This chapter looked at current research that has identified factors that can place youth at elevated risk for considering suicide. These risk factors, described as the yellow lights on the traffic signal of youth suicide indicators, help direct our attention to things in a student's life that can be modified to lessen suicide risk. The red lights on that traffic signal are the warning signs that indicate a youth may be at immediate or elevated suicide risk. The rationale for presenting this information is to dispel the myth that we are helpless to prevent suicide. By recognizing youth who may be struggling with risk factors or actually presenting warning signs and referring them to appropriate mental health resources for additional assessment and intervention, school staff members have an important role to play in suicide prevention. The next chapters will describe how—using this information about risk factors and warning signs as a foundation—school resource staff can gather additional data to make the most effective possible referral for students who require community-based interventions.

IN YOUR
## Experience . . .

- Can you identify students who exhibit risk factors for suicide?
- Have you observed risk factors that have been changed—for example, students who got treatment for mental health or substance abuse problems? How did this seem to affect their suicide risk?
- If you've known students who have made suicide attempts, can you identify what the warning signs may have been?

**Chapter 4**  Identification: Who Are the Students Who Might Be At Risk?

**59**

## RESOURCES

Aseltine Jr., R. H., and R. DeMartino. "An Outcome Evaluation of the SOS Suicide Prevention Program." *American Journal of Public Health* 94, no. 3 (2004): 446–51.

Berman, A. L. "School-based Suicide Prevention: Research Advances and Practice Implications." *School Psychology Review* 38 no. 2 (2009): 233–38.

Gould, M. S., F. A. Marrocco, M. Kleinman, J. Thomas, K. Mostkoff, J. Cote, and M. Davies. "Evaluating Iatrogenic Risk of Youth Suicide Screening Programs: A Randomized Controlled Trial." *Journal of the American Medical Association* 293 no. 13 (2005): 1635–43.

King, C. A., N. Ghaziuddin, L. McGovern, E. Brand, E. Hill, and M. Naylor. "Predictors of Comorbid Alcohol and Substance Abuse in Depressed Adolescents." *Journal of the American Academy of Child and Adolescent Psychiatry* 35 no. 6 (1996): 743–51.

King, K. A., and J. Smith. "Project SOAR: A Training Program to Increase School Counselors' Knowledge and Confidence Regarding Suicide Prevention and Intervention." *Journal of School Health* 70 no. 10 (2000): 402.

Rudd, M. D., A. L. Berman, T. E. Joiner, M. K. Nock, M. Silverman, M. Mandrusiak, K. Van Orden, and T. Witte. "Warning Signs for Suicide: Theory, Research, and Clinical Applications." *Suicide and Life-Threatening Behavior* 36 no. 3 (2006): 255–62.

Ushkow, M. C., J. R. Asbury, B. Bradford, P. R. Nader, S. R. Poole, D. Worthington, A. B. Elster, V. Haines, P. W. Jung, P. Lachelt, R. D. Legako, J. Santelli, and J. H. Williams. "The Potentially Suicidal Student in the School Setting." *Pediatrics* 86 no. 3 (1990): 481.

## HANDOUTS

4-1: FACTS

# Chapter 5

..........................................................................................................

# Setting the Stage: Preparing for the Assessment Interview

*"Asking about suicide is never easy. But after a student in our school made a very serious attempt, it sure got easier for me. I realized that maybe, just maybe, I might be the one to help a student get enough professional support to realize there are healthier ways to solve problems. And the easier it got for me to ask questions about suicide, the easier it seemed to be for students to answer."*

—*STUDENT ASSISTANCE COUNSELOR*

As you've seen from the previous chapters, the foundation for an effective assessment interview is set long before you are sitting across the desk from a potentially at-risk student. While much has been written about suicide risk assessment in clinical mental health settings, it's hard to find information tailored to the critical but limited role the school often plays in this process. Although the clinical assessment is very important, it often isn't the place where the intervention starts. Youth are frequently first identified in the school setting where the changes in a student's behavior may be most evident. So regardless of the extent of the initial interview in the school, school is really the place where intervention begins.

Certainly, talking about suicide is never either easy or routine, so this chapter will provide pointers to make you feel more comfortable with the process. The assessment/intervention process itself has four components:

1. Preparation for the interview
2. Interview with the student

Lifelines Intervention
. . . . . . . . . . . . . . . . . . . . . . . . . . . . . . . . . . . . . . . . . . . . . . . . . . . . . . . . . . . . . . . . . . . . . . . . . . . . . . . . .

**62**

**3.** Parental contact

**4.** Referral

Each of these components is extremely important. The way the initial student intervention is handled can set the stage for helping both the student and his or her parents realize and accept that further assessment is needed. This chapter will review information to keep in mind as you prepare to interview a student, the first component of the process. It will provide a framework to help you approach the interview as well as highlight key aspects of developmental theory to consider in planning your interventions with elementary, middle, and high school students. Finally, it will provide practical examples of questioning techniques that you can adapt to your own personal interviewing style.

By the end of this chapter, you will be able to

- understand the key components of an effective assessment

- know what key counseling techniques to use in an assessment interview

- list specific developmentally appropriate strategies for interviewing children and adolescents

## I'VE LOOKED AT MY PERSONAL ATTITUDES AND VALUES ABOUT SUICIDE. WHAT ELSE DO I NEED TO KNOW BEFORE I'M PREPARED FOR AN INTERVIEW WITH A STUDENT?

The place to start is with a clear understanding of what you want to accomplish in the interview. Knowing your goals beforehand is one of the best ways to help you organize your thinking so that you can accomplish these goals. In most school settings, the primary goal of an assessment interview is to determine whether the student is presenting with suicide risk and if that is the case, to facilitate a referral to community mental health resources for a more complete assessment. Depending on the nature of the referral for assessment, secondary goals may arise during the course of the interview itself. These can include giving feedback to the classroom teacher on supporting the student, providing information to a treating therapist about the student's behaviors in the school setting, and helping the student understand why a mental health referral may be needed. As you can see, a lot of additional action items can emerge from this one interview.

In most schools, the staff members who conduct these interviews are not in a position to, nor are they expected to, develop a clinical diagnosis of the student. Making a differential diagnosis of mental disorders in youth is a complicated process that is almost impossible to accomplish in a single interview. Seasoned mental health professionals usually formulate diagnoses over the course of several interviews, with input not just from the student and his or her family but from ancillary sources as well. In some schools, however, school resource staff such as psychologists and social workers have the training to make a provisional diagnosis that they may include as part of the referral to outside resources. The key point to remember, however, is that the school is not a mental health center. The assessment interview in the school opens the door to a referral for more comprehensive mental health evaluation by an off-campus resource.

Preparing for an intervention with a student, especially when you are addressing something as serious as potential suicide risk, is crucial. The best preparation starts at a generic level with an understanding of the basic principles of a risk assessment interview. These principles are derived from the more clinical assessments that take place in mental health settings, but, as you will see, the principles can be modified to the assessments done in a school.

Suicide assessment isn't just an interview; it's a process. If there is enough concern about a student to warrant a referral for a suicide assessment, then this student needs to stay on your radar, regardless of the outcome of your initial assessment. Just the fact that the student was referred for assessment raises a red flag. It tells you that something might be going on that requires intervention. While you may not feel the student is currently at risk for suicide, you will want to keep your eyes and ears open for signs that his or her distress has escalated and another intervention might be warranted.

There's another reason for continued observation in the context of process assessment. Often when schools refer students to mental health facilities for what they feel is high suicidal risk that requires immediate hospitalization, they are dismayed when the student is back at school the next day. In most cases, there has been a determination that the student's level of risk can be managed in a less restrictive setting like outpatient treatment. In other cases, however, the information shared by the student and his or her family doesn't capture what's been observed by the school. The more information you have to support your concerns, the better chance you have of assisting the student in getting the help he or she needs. If you consider your assessments from the perspective of a process, you can continue to gather data to make a more convincing case for hospitalization in the future if it still seems indicated.

Avoid clichés. Although it is undoubtedly true that suicide *is* a permanent solution to a temporary problem, this cliché tends to minimize the gravity of the distress a person must feel to be considering suicide as a viable option. Particularly with teens, who may feel adults do not understand their lives or experiences, this worn cliché confirms the ignorance of adults.

*"Yeah sure, my parents never liked Tiffany, but she was everything to me. The only one who really understood me or cared. So when she dumped me, it DID feel like my world ended. I truly wanted to die. And they give me this line about how I'll find somebody else, tomorrow's another day, blah, blah, blah . . . Are they kidding me or what?"*

—SOPHOMORE BOY

It's so much more supportive to explain that sometimes in life the world as we have known it *does* end, and although it can take a while, with understanding and support we can figure out how to go on. It's essentially the same message about suicide being a permanent solution but said in a kinder way that doesn't insult or discount emotional pain the way a cliché sometimes can.

Since the goal of the interview is to assess suicide risk, it must include direct questions about suicide. There is an unfortunate myth that asking about suicide can plant the idea in the mind of a vulnerable student. Research and experience have demonstrated that this is simply not the case. Many people feel they have to keep suicidal thoughts a secret because, as we have seen in chapter 2, suicide is such a stigmatized topic. For youth in particular, the weight of a secret about suicide can be heavy and isolating. It's not uncommon for suicidal youth to feel like they are the only ones in the world who have ever felt this way. A considerable amount of evidence actually suggests that suicidal people are relieved when someone brings up what has felt like a forbidden topic.

Talking about suicidal thoughts and feelings—with the right person—can make all the difference in the world. Mary Karr's poem "Incant Against Suicide" makes the point in a simple, direct way youth can understand. "Your head's a bad neighborhood," she writes, "don't go there alone."

Karr speaks a universal truth. When we're in scary places—whether they're bad neighborhoods or the dark corners of our minds—we're always better off when we've got someone there with us who tries to understand us and help us figure out what to do to get out of danger.

Finally, the essential element of all student contact: documentation. Mental health clinicians have a saying: if it wasn't written down, it didn't happen.

This saying sums up just about everything you need to know about documentation. The written recording of what took place between you and the student doesn't have to be long or detailed. It merely needs to reference the important points in the interview, outline your recommendations, indicate your communication with the student's parents or guardians, and be dated and signed by you. It

## Response to the Myth That Talking about Suicide with Kids Will "Plant the Idea"
### by John Kalafat, Ph.D.

There are several arguments in response to this myth:

Talking about suicide will not plant the idea in teens' heads because they are already well aware of suicide from their experiences with suicidal peers and from things they have been exposed to in the media.[1]

Over the course of thirty years of hotline experience and twenty years of school-based suicide prevention programming, I have never encountered a case of planting the idea of suicide. The Centers for Disease Control and Prevention has clearly stated this:

> There is no evidence of increased suicide ideation or behavior among program participants . . .[2] Furthermore, numerous research and intervention efforts have been completed without any reports of harm.[3]

There have been several evaluations of school-based programs that show increased likelihood that program participants will tell an adult about a suicidal peer or will report suicidal thoughts as compared with controls.[4]

Lastly, there have also been two long-term follow-up studies in counties where suicide prevention programs were provided in nearly all county schools over a period of years that show reductions in youth suicide rates.[5]

1. See J. Kalafat and M. Elias, "Adolescents' Experience with and Response to Suicidal Peers," *Suicide and Life-Threatening Behavior* 22 (1992): 315–21.

2. See *Youth Suicide Prevention Programs: A Resource Guide* (Atlanta, GA: Centers for Disease Control, 1992), 66.

3. See L. Potter, K. E. Powell, and S. P. Kacher, "Suicide Prevention from a Mental Health Perspective," *Suicide and Life-Threatening Behavior* 11 (1995): 25.

4. See J. Ciffone, "Suicide Prevention: A Classroom Presentation to Adolescents," *Social Work* 38 (1993): 196–203. L. L. Eggert, E. A. Thompson, J. R. Herting, and L. J. Nicholas, "Reducing Suicide Potential among High School Youth: Tests of a School-based Program," *Suicide and Life-Threatening Behavior* 25 (1995): 276–96. J. Kalafat and M. Elias, "An Evaluation of Suicide Intervention Classes," *Suicide and Life-Threatening Behavior* 24 (1994): 224–33. J. Kalafat and C. Gagliano, "The Use of Simulations to Assess the Impact of an Adolescent Suicide Response Curriculum," *Suicide and Life-Threatening Behavior* 26 (1996): 359–64. I. Orbach and H. Bar-Joseph, "The Impact of a Suicide Prevention Program for Adolescents on Suicidal Tendencies, Hopelessness, Ego Identity, and Coping," *Suicide and Life-Threatening Behavior* 23 (1993): 120–29.

5. See J. Kalafat and D. Ryerson, "The Implementation and Institutionalization of a School-based Youth Suicide Prevention Program," *Journal of Primary Prevention* 19 (1999): 157-75. F. J. Zenere and P. J. Lazarus, "The Decline of Youth Suicidal Behavior in an Urban, Multicultural Public School System Following the Introduction of a Suicide Prevention and Intervention Program," *Suicide and Life-Threatening Behavior* 4 (1997): 387–403.

*Note: This article reprinted from www.sptsusa.org.*

should also include a timeline for follow-up. (See Documentation of Suicide Risk on the CD-ROM.) This written record protects you and the school in the event that there any questions about the assessment at a later time.

Here's a review of the key components of assessment:

- Know the personal characteristics you bring to the assessment.
- Consider the individuality, cultural background, and developmental level of each student.
- Integrate collaboration into every part of the process.
- Ask direct questions about suicide.
- Remember to follow up.
- Don't use clichés.
- Document!
- Remember to follow up on the effectiveness of the community referral.

School assessments also draw upon your own skills and experience, the individuality of the student, and collaborative efforts with parents and community resources.

## WHAT DO I BRING TO THE INTERVIEW?

You are as significant to the interview as the questions you ask. Not only do you bring your attitudes and personal values about suicide; you also bring your interviewing skills and experience. Your previous contact with the student is a factor, too. Each of these elements adds a dimension to the process that can affect its outcome. That's why it's important to consider each of these personal aspects prior to beginning any assessment. In chapter 2 we discussed your personal values, attitudes, and experiences with suicide. Here we are talking about the interview skills and experience you bring to the intervention. Ask yourself these questions:

- Have I assessed suicide risk in students before?
- What aspects of that process were challenging for me?
- What personal and professional skills do I bring to this interview?
- What can I do to help the student feel comfortable?

## WHAT DOES THE STUDENT BRING TO THE INTERVIEW?

Consider the situation from the student's perspective: I am being told I have to go to this adult whom I may or may not even know to get help for a personal problem I may not even understand or want to talk about. That's the way the stage is set for a lot of kids. In fact, when students have been asked in general how they feel about asking adults for help with their problems, their responses usually have been negative. In addition to feeling that adults don't understand their feelings, they worry that adults don't take them seriously or even listen to what they have to say. Teens also admit that they think they'll be perceived as "crazy" or "weak" if they talk about disturbing thoughts like suicide.

Given this general adolescent mind-set, students may be very apprehensive about self-disclosure, especially when it relates to suicide. When it comes to talking to the school counselor, teens may put themselves in a classic "lose-lose" situation: reluctant to talk to a stranger or someone they don't know but embarrassed to talk to someone who does know them.

Teens may have the same misconceptions about mental health and the counseling process as many adults do. They may be frightened about the potential outcome of this discussion with a school counselor, worried about the reactions of their parents, or scared that they may be hospitalized. Some students, though, may be relieved to get help in handling the situation that is creating such overwhelming distress for them.

### How Students May Feel about Asking Adults for Help

- Concerned that adults don't understand their feelings
- Reluctant because they don't think adults listen to them
- Worried they will be seen as crazy or weak
- Confused about mental health or the counseling process
- Scared about parental reactions or being hospitalized
- Relieved

## HOW DO I KNOW WHAT THE STUDENT SITTING ACROSS FROM ME IS THINKING OR FEELING?

Ask! If you remember the principle of the assessment process about the uniqueness and individuality of each student, you'll realize that the above examples of student reactions to adults are just that—merely examples of the range of feelings students may experience. By simply asking, "How do you feel about talking with me today?" and really noticing and listening to the student's verbal and nonverbal responses, you'll get a good idea of where to begin.

*"Tajir was referred by his homeroom teacher who was concerned after she had overheard him saying to another student that he planned to take his life. As soon as he sat down for the interview, his body language made it clear he didn't want to be there. He looked around the room, then at his watch, then over at me with a blank expression on his face. He knew why I had been asked to talk with him—his teacher had told him of her concern—so I decided to cut to the chase in my opening line by asking 'So tell me why you don't want to be here.' And tell me he did! For almost 10 minutes. After that, he seemed to relax and we talked productively for almost 45 minutes."*

—SCHOOL SOCIAL WORKER

## HOW CAN A STUDENT'S CULTURAL BACKGROUND AFFECT THE INTERVIEW?

Being sensitive to a student's cultural background is essential in any interaction, but it is especially significant when addressing issues of suicide risk. In some cultures, for example, an act of suicide is an honorable way to atone for wrongdoing. Other cultures view mental illness as a punishment for sin or deny it entirely. This cultural context is one of the reasons it can be helpful to avoid labeling any of the student's behaviors as indicative of mental illness. That discussion is better left to the mental health professional to whom you are making a referral. Of course, if you are aware of the meaning of both suicide and mental illness to a particular student, you can incorporate that understanding into your preparation. If your school population is extremely diverse, however, this level of personal understanding might be impossible. In that case, you can simply incorporate questions that address the cultural context into your interview. For example, you might say, "I know that all cultures do not view suicide in the same way. Can you tell me how it is viewed from your background?"

# HOW DOES A STUDENT'S DEVELOPMENTAL LEVEL AFFECT THE INTERVIEW PROCESS?

As someone who works in a school setting, you realize the importance of considering the students' developmental and maturity levels in relation to their ability to understand and participate in the assessment process. The best assessment questions and techniques will be useless unless adapted to a student's level of comprehension.

You'll have a great baseline for approaching an assessment interview by remembering how you already incorporate your knowledge about the developmental and maturity level of students into all of your interactions. Keeping these concepts in mind is even more important when you're approaching a difficult topic like suicide. The following section briefly reviews key aspects of development that are relevant to the interview process.

## *Elementary School Students*

Although the suicide risk for this age group of students is very low, you may find yourself receiving referrals for students who talk about wanting to die or kill themselves. With children in this age bracket, it's important to remember that, for the most part, they are eager to please the adults in their lives. If you ask questions in a way that suggests you expect a certain answer, the young student may give you the answer he or she thinks you want, whether or not it is true.

> *Counselor:* You don't really mean that you want to die, do you?
>
> *Student:* No, ma'am.

Phrasing questions in a way that provides the student with the choice of responses tends to yield an honest answer.

> *Counselor:* I want to be sure I understand what you're telling me.
>   Do you want to die or do you just want to feel better?
>
> *Student:* I think I really want to die.

This interaction also demonstrates another point: use simple, clear words. While the word "suicide" is often used interchangeably with "wanting to die," the latter expression is simpler for young children to understand.

Because younger children are also concrete, literal thinkers, be sure to be specific in your word choices. For example, if you ask a child, "Do you want to hurt yourself?" you may get a negative response if the child is thinking about wanting to die. A useful sequencing of questions for younger children might start with questions about self-harm and move to questions about taking one's life. And remember, just because a child responds negatively about self-harm does not mean he or she isn't thinking about dying.

*"When I asked nine-year-old Cameron if he thought about suicide, he said no, even though he'd told his teacher he wanted to jump off his roof and die. So I asked him if he understood the word 'suicide,' and he said, yes, it meant hanging yourself, which is what his uncle did. He didn't want to do that, he said, because he didn't know how. He just wanted to die and he thought jumping off his roof was the way to make this happen."*

—ELEMENTARY SCHOOL PSYCHOLOGIST

Providing examples to clarify the intent of your questions can also be helpful for younger children. If you are asking, for example, how often a child has thoughts about dying, provide some time frames and, if you know about them, what appear to be triggering events.

> *Counselor:* So when you tell me, Tyler, that you think about dying "a lot," how often is "a lot"? Is it every day, every now and then, or whenever you get into a fight with your parents?

Parental reaction is an especially big concern for most elementary school children, who may be worried about how their parents or guardians will react to these disclosures. Be as honestly reassuring as you can be. Say that you will talk with the student's caretakers to help them understand what's been going on. Note the use of the words *as honestly reassuring as you can be.* While it would also be reassuring to every school counselor to think that all the adults in a child's life will be understanding and supportive, this is, unfortunately, not always the case. Here's an example of a statement that gently reflects this honest reality:

> *Counselor:* I promise you, Tyler, that I will do my best to help your parents understand what you've been going through.

It can also be useful to solicit the student's opinion about ways to approach his or her parents. Engaging the child in the problem-solving process helps him or her to move away from feelings of helplessness to feelings of empowerment.

> *Counselor:* You know your parents better than I do, Tyler. Give me
> some suggestions about how we can talk to them about
> this. For example, which one of your parents is easier
> for you to talk with—your mom or your dad?

Recognize that all children, but particularly younger ones, need to feel supported during the interview process. Remind them often that you understand how hard it can be to talk about personal feelings, especially with someone they don't know very well, and that they're doing a great job in helping you understand how they've been feeling lately.

Sometimes elementary school students find it easier to talk about personal feelings if a teacher whom they trust is present during the interview. Especially if you, as the counselor, have had only minimal contact with the student, it can be very helpful to invite another faculty member who knows the student to sit in on the discussion. Not only does it provide the student with the comforting presence of a familiar face, it also models the usefulness of getting support from as many people as you can when you feel distressed.

*"I had never met Thomas before and he seemed really reluctant to say anything to me except 'yes' or 'no' or 'I don't know.' I knew I wasn't getting anywhere so I asked him if he'd like me to invite his teacher to sit with us since she knew him really well and might be able to help him think through the answers to some of my questions, which I knew could be really hard. His face brightened and it told me that was fine with him. Well, as soon as she entered the room, the climate changed and the interview got on track."*

—*SCHOOL COUNSELOR*

## Middle School Students

You will have no trouble recognizing middle school as the bridge of transition in a student's life between the security of elementary school and the relative freedom of high school. For many kids, being on that bridge means leaving behind the schedule and routine that organized the school day, the friends who may now go to different middle schools, and, for good or bad, the teachers who knew their names.

For students, the transition to middle school can be scary. Kids express worries about not being able to get to class on time or keep up with homework. They can be overwhelmed by having to organize their lockers and adjust to different teachers with different levels of expectations, and they can be totally panicked by having to find people to sit with at lunch.

Middle school students also experience strong, often conflicting, emotions and social pressures as they move away from childhood toward more independent young adulthood. Drama and emotional outbursts are the name of the game for many of these kids. In addition to the physical changes that signal puberty is under way, we also see an increase in the prevalence of depression, especially among girls. Prior to puberty there are no gender differences in the depression rates. But with the onset of puberty, the rate in females increases, with a female to male ratio of 2 to 1. Increases in hormones, changes in body shape, and emerging sexual identity may predispose adolescent girls to depression. Although depression is only one of the risk factors for suicide, it can make all the normal challenges of adolescence a lot harder. Fragile self-esteem is compromised, thinking is impaired, and peer relationships can seem like too much work for too little reward.

One of the biggest challenges to suicide prevention and assessment in middle school is peer allegiance. This replaces elementary school students' reliance on adults. Too many kids say that they would keep the confidence of a *suicidal peer* rather than confide that information in a *trusted adult*. Although middle school students assume that what happens in their peer relationships is under adult radar, the drama of their interactions often makes their "private" lives public. Interestingly, referrals for potentially at-risk students begin to come from peers in middle school, especially if the peers feel overwhelmed with the burden of keeping the confidence of their suicidal peer. When you receive this type of referral, it's generally preferable not to betray the confidence of the referral source. This will increase the chances that other students will feel comfortable coming to you with their concerns about peers or about themselves. While most referred students will have a good idea which friends alerted the counselor to their distress, the interview needs to remain focused on the *reasons* for the referral and not the referral *source*.

> **Student:** I want you to tell me which one of my friends told you I thought about taking those pills.

> **Counselor:** It doesn't matter who told me. What's important here is that your friends are concerned about you and so am I. I really want to know what was going on last week that made you feel so bad you talked about taking pills and dying.

The counselor keeps the focus on what really needs to be addressed in the interview: the possible suicidal behavior. He or she reframes the fact that the student's friends made the referral to counseling as an example of their concern, which the counselor shares.

We also have to be careful not to allow the need of middle schoolers to assert their budding independence to adversely affect our assessment techniques. While the options for personal decision making certainly increase from elementary to middle school, deciding whether or not to participate in a counseling interview is not one of them. Check out the differences in the following statements:

| COUNSELOR 1: | COUNSELOR 2: |
|---|---|
| Hey, Jasmine—thanks for coming down to talk with me. There's something that a couple of your teachers have brought to my attention that I'd like to chat with you about. How does that sound to you? | Hi, Jasmine. Take a seat. There are a few things I'd like to talk with you about today. Could you close the door so we can have some privacy? |

Counselor 1 is definitely more informal and conversational, but Jasmine could be left with the impression that she has a choice about whether the interview takes place. Counselor 2 makes it clear that the decision remains with the counselor, not Jasmine. It is, of course, one of the paradoxes of early adolescence that, as much as young teens protest the control of adults, they need to know it's still very much in place in order to feel safe in their forays into independence. Especially when students are struggling with unfamiliar or upsetting emotions, knowing that an adult is still in charge is critical to establishing an interview climate that facilitates safe discussion about possible suicide risk.

The counselor's authority must, of course, be tempered with patience. This can often take the form of waiting quietly for a student to answer a question rather than filling the silence with another question that you hope the student is more inclined to answer. "Waiting out the silence" is a strategic interviewing technique that again demonstrates who is in charge. Most students will ultimately provide some answer if you wait long enough. However, if you're dealing with a resistant student whose silence goes on for what feels like forever, try interrupting with a statement like this: "I can see you're really thinking about your response. I appreciate that you're taking this so seriously." This will usually provoke some type of reaction, demonstrate that you are still in charge, and open the door to further conversation.

Finally, even though middle school students can sometimes be melodramatic, take all talk about suicide seriously—even if you've heard it before. If a student is in your office multiple times for making comments about suicide or other self-destructive behavior, some type of counseling is needed to figure out why the student's problem solving is so compromised. In these situations, more parental involvement is usually warranted as well. Remember, even when students present with concern about suicide risk on multiple occasions, their parents must be contacted *every time* the issue is raised. You must also document each instance with the same diligence and care. While this can be frustrating at times, it serves as your legal protection in case there is ever any question about the school's response to a potentially at-risk student, and it may also be the time you save a student's life.

*"Ryan was in my office at least seven times, referred by a faculty or staff member who was concerned about Ryan's self-destructive behavior or comments. Each time I called his parents, they took him to their pediatrician who would say there was no reason for concern. After the fifth time or so, his mother got really angry with me for making such a big deal out of nothing. What could I say? I told her it was school policy and I was obligated to both let her know and insist Ryan be seen by a professional who could clear him to return to school. After the seventh time, the parents took him to a psychologist instead of the pediatrician. He recommended counseling and an evaluation for medication. And Ryan hasn't been referred to me again!"*

—SCHOOL NURSE

### High School Students

High school students, especially freshmen and sophomores, may still be struggling intensely with separation/individuation issues, so you may need some of the same interview techniques you use with middle school adolescents. It's even more important to do your homework before you talk with an older teen to make sure you've got as clear a picture as possible about the reasons for referral. Behaviorally specific examples of situations that have sounded the alarm bells about this particular student are much more effective and convincing than vague, generalized statements about concern. It's harder for students to argue with facts.

*"Anderson was pretty belligerent when I called him down to my office to talk to him. He said he was fine, there was nothing going on, and everyone should mind their own business. When I said that there seemed to be a few things going on, and then listed them—like his grade had dropped from a C to an F in history, he was about to lose credit for his first-period math class because he had been absent so much, he'd had*

*four detentions for being disrespectful to his teachers in the past two months—well, he got a little less angry and said there were some personal things going on he didn't want to get into. When I responded that he could keep them personal, I just wanted to know what the school could do to help him, he started to cry."*

*—SCHOOL COUNSELOR*

This example also demonstrates another principle of effective interviewing, especially in high school: don't be intimidated. If the counselor isn't careful, the anger of students like Anderson who approach the counselor with a chip on their shoulders can set the interview tone. As with middle school students, the issue is remaining in charge of the interview, not giving control to the student. An interview that is dominated by a student's intimidating anger is doomed.

It can help to remember that intimidation is often a defensive tactic used by a student who is probably waiting to be attacked and is taking the first shot with his or her hostile attitude. The easiest way to undercut intimidation is to ignore it as this counselor did. Then he skillfully outlined all the data he had collected about Anderson's current school performance. This information spelled out clearly the reason for the school's concern to defuse the boy's claims that everything in his life was okay.

The corollary to the principle of not being intimidated is to not be intimidating yourself. It helps to remember that for many students, a summons to the counselor's office is in itself frightening. Your attitude does not need to increase student fear. Rather, it should do the opposite—lessen the fear so the student feels comfortable and safe discussing his or her personal concerns.

Some counselors can be intimidating without even realizing it. Men, in fact, generally tend to be seen as more intimidating than women, especially if they are large in frame and stature. In addition, a counselor who seems abrupt, distracted, or preoccupied can be perceived as intimidating because students may have difficulty connecting with him or her and establishing rapport. The reverse is also true: a counselor who seems overengaged in the students' problems may be equally intimidating. Students may fear this counselor's overintrusiveness.

*"You might have thought that Ms. G was the kind of counselor every kid wanted to have—always there for you, remembering important dates in your life. But a couple of my friends had to go see her for problems at school and they said she was a nightmare. I mean, like they figured out what to do and she talked with their parents and everything, but she would not let it go. She kept calling them down to the office to 'check on' them, calling their parents to see how stuff was going at home. She like never let up! It got so bad one of them went to the assistant principal to ask if he could get another counselor."*

—JUNIOR BOY

Another important thing to remember is to ask students to explain what they mean when they use certain terms, and for you to do the same. Even if you are well-versed in adolescent jargon, never assume you know the meaning of all expressions. It does not diminish your credibility as a "cool" counselor to say: "I think I know what you mean by that, but would you mind explaining it to me to make sure I understand your meaning?"

Most of the words you need to use carefully are those that explain feelings or mental health terms. It isn't patronizing or demeaning to ask a student if he or she understands what you are talking about. Consider this:

> *Counselor:* It sounds, Hannah, like you've been pretty apathetic lately.
>
> *Hannah:* No way, I don't have an eating disorder!
>
> *Counselor:* I'm confused. I didn't say that.
>
> *Hannah:* You just did. You said I am apathetic. Isn't that an eating disorder?
>
> *Counselor:* Oh. No. that's anorexic.

It's essential to clarify the subtleties in the language of feelings, especially when you are dealing with students for whom English is a second language. What is very evident to you may be lost on students whose feelings vocabularies are often limited to being "bored." It's also important not to toss around mental health diagnoses like depression, bipolar disorder, attention deficit disorder, and so on. Even if a student seems to clearly exhibit the symptoms of a particular mental disorder, diagnosis of that disorder is not your job. However, you can suggest that the off-campus mental health professional to whom you are referring investigate possible symptoms of depression, and so on.

## HOW DOES PREVIOUS CONTACT WITH THE STUDENT AFFECT THE INTERVIEW PROCESS?

We would all like to say that we don't have favorites in the student population or that there aren't students whose very shadows make us want to close our doors. However, it's unrealistic to believe we don't have stronger connections to some students than to others. If you think of your current relationships with the students in your school, for example, you'll realize that previous contact can have an impact on the assessment interview in both positive and negative ways. Take a look at the chart below.

### Previous Contact with the Student

| Potential Positives | Potential Negatives |
|---|---|
| You may have a better idea of what to expect from the student. | If your previous contact with the student has been negative, you may begin the interview with a negative mind-set. |
| Rapport with the student may already exist or be easy to establish. | Rapport may not exist or the student may refuse to cooperate with you. |
| Previous knowledge of the student may provide perspective for current information. | Remaining objective about the current situation may be difficult. If you are close to the student, you may be personally affected by his or her thoughts about suicide. If you know the student to be overly dramatic, you may be somewhat dismissive of suicidal concerns. |
| Problem solving may be quicker and more targeted to the student's personal situation. | Your previous history with the student may predetermine the outcome of the contact. |

## HOW DOES NOT HAVING HAD PREVIOUS CONTACT AFFECT THE INTERVIEW?

It may be easier to bring objectivity to an interview with a student whom you don't know. However, establishing the rapport necessary to engage the student in discussion about suicide may be more challenging. In these situations, you'll have to rely almost entirely on secondhand information to put the student's issues into context, so gathering collateral information will be especially important. The good news, however, is that your problem solving will be focused on the situation at hand and not clouded by previous contact.

## WHAT DO YOU MEAN BY "COLLABORATION"?

Collaboration is essential to a comprehensive assessment and includes a partnership between the school, the student, the family, and the community mental health resources to which you are making a referral for more detailed assessment. Before you interview a student, your process should start with gathering specific information from the referral source about the reasons for concern about a particular student. You can include statements in your assessment such as "Your teachers have told me that your grades are dropping and you've seemed totally disinterested in what's going on in the classroom. You are a good student and they're concerned about you." In addition, having specific, behaviorally observable data about the student's attitude and behavior outside of the interview situation gives you more to work with if the student is noncompliant or denies problems. Compare the differences in these two interactions:

| |  |
|---|---|
| **COUNSELOR:** There's been some concern about the way you've been acting lately.<br><br>**STUDENT:** What do you mean?<br><br>**COUNSELOR:** You're not yourself. And you made that comment about thinking about killing yourself.<br><br>**STUDENT:** I was being dramatic. Anyone who knows me will tell you that's just how I am. | **COUNSELOR:** I've talked with some of your teachers and they said your grades have been dropping for the last month. For example, you've gone from a B in English to a D. You've also stopped turning in biology assignments and have been coming late to your first period class at least twice a week. We're concerned about these changes. What's up? |

Simply put, the more supporting data you have to back up your reasons for being concerned about the student, the more credibility the interview will have. In some schools, it may be difficult to get this kind of specificity. But it doesn't hurt to try to get some idea of the reasons for concerns about the student. Examples of strategies for eliciting this information from teachers and other school-based referral sources can be found in chapter 6.

## HOW DO YOU GATHER BACKGROUND INFORMATION WHEN THE REFERRAL IS FROM A PEER?

It's important to think about this so you can be prepared to address referrals from other students, especially in schools that have implemented a suicide prevention curriculum that encourages students to take some responsibility for each other's welfare. In these situations, ask the specific reasons for the peer's concerns just as you would when the referral is from a faculty or staff member. Usually peers will give you very clear and direct explanations ("He's talking about wanting to die," "She's getting really wasted at parties," or "She made an attempt last year and she's acting the way she did then"). Even when the reason for peer referral is vague ("She's just not herself lately"), what makes these referrals especially important is their source: peers who know the student. Peers tend to evaluate each other in terms of their relevant behavioral norms. They know when someone is acting in a way that isn't "normal" for their age group or not like himself or herself. Always take peer referrals very seriously. This is an example of when the source of the referral is as important as its content. You can respect confidentiality ("Some of the other students are concerned about you") and zero in on the fact that when peers are concerned about each other, you always follow up.

## Peer Referrals for Cutting and Other Self-harm

A frequent reason for peer referral is for friends who are cutting, self-harming, or self-injuring. Sometimes the friend will have told peers about the behavior, but, as often as not, peers will have observed the friend's cuts or other signs of self-injury in gym class or elsewhere. The motivation for self-injury is generally not to die; it is more often a learned coping mechanism that relieves emotional distress. Cutting brings elevated levels of psychological and physiological tension back to bearable levels through the endorphins released to address the physical pain caused by the injury. Students who self-injure tend to have limited feelings vocabularies, which means they have difficulty expressing either personal needs or emotions. Self-injury becomes a behavior that provides initial emotional relief, but, unfortunately, it often becomes a habit. Although the intent of self-injury may not be suicidal, it is nonetheless a serious problem that requires a referral to an off-campus mental health professional for further evaluation and treatment recommendations.

> **Collaborative Partners**
>
> - School-based referral source (teachers, peers, etc.)
> - Student
> - Parents
> - Community referral resource (for example, a mental health agency)

You also want to develop a collaborative relationship with the student you are interviewing. Remember that feeling suicidal is an isolating experience. Children and teens can feel very alone in the emotional confusion, frustration, and desperation that accompany thoughts of suicide. Being able to convince students through your language and demeanor that you're emotionally available to share their pain and to collaborate with them on finding a better solution than suicide is a critical element for a successful intervention. Having the student's parents as a part of the collaborative team also can make the difference in achieving a positive outcome. Chapter 7 discusses the process of collaborating with parents.

*"Erin's parents were pretty upset when I asked them to come in to talk about her risk for suicide. What helped me convince them they needed to take Erin for further evaluation was the fact that I had talked to them in the past about their concerns about Erin's grades. They knew me, they trusted me, and they knew that I knew Erin."*

—GUIDANCE COUNSELOR

Finally, collaboration also includes the community mental health resources to which you are making a referral for more detailed assessment. Since the school is only the initial part of assessment, having a pre-existing working relationship with your referral resources, such as the memorandum of understanding discussed in chapter 1, can streamline the process and better ensure that the student gets the services he or she needs. It's also useful to ask the parents/guardians to sign a release so the community referral resource can share limited information with the school to assist in creating an environment that supports the student's treatment plan. This limited information can lead to adjustments in school such as providing additional time for the completion of assignments until medication treatment is stabilized, setting up regular conferences with guidance staff to review the student's status and progress, and so on.

## WHAT COLLATERAL INFORMATION CAN SCHOOL SOURCES PROVIDE?

Think of collateral information as any type of data that supports the school's concerns about a particular student. Information that would be helpful to know prior to conducting an assessment interview includes the following:

- recent changes in the student's schoolwork
- differences in behavior, attitudes, or emotions (ask for examples)
- disruptive, disrespectful, or troublesome behaviors
- detention or suspension history
- current peer relationships
- attendance records
- verbal threats of suicide or preoccupation with themes of death and destruction in schoolwork
- concerns expressed by peers

The challenge, of course, is that it takes time to gather this information, and most referrals for an assessment of suicide risk are received on an emergency basis. Although you can generally get some information from the referral source, you will most likely go into the interview not knowing everything that could be useful in your assessment. If you can, continue to gather data after the interview so you can pass it along to the referral resource or keep it in your files as you follow up with this student over time. Let school staff know to check in with you if there are any changes in the student's behavior—in either a positive or negative direction.

## NOW THAT I KNOW THIS, WHAT TECHNIQUES ARE HELPFUL WHEN INTERVIEWING A STUDENT ABOUT SUICIDE RISK?

The basics of good interviewing obviously apply to every counseling or intervention situation; however, a couple of points deserve to be highlighted because they are even more important when discussing an emotionally laden topic like suicide with a student. Helpful guidelines for interviewing students include

- Clarify the meanings of words
- Stay in control of the interview
- Be patient
- Don't intimidate or be intimidated
- Provide specific examples of behaviors that cause concern
- Involve the student in problem solving

- Take every instance of possible suicide risk seriously
- Use collateral information

5-2

The chart below lists specific techniques to keep in mind in doing a suicide assessment interview. It also explains why these techniques are effective and provides examples of how to translate them into conversational statements. A copy of this chart can also be found on the CD-ROM.

# Student Assessment Interview Chart

| What to Do | Why It Works | What to Say |
|---|---|---|
| Prepare for the interview. Get collateral information, review student's records, hold all phone calls, have tissues available. | Even if you have only 5 minutes to get organized for the interview, your preparation demonstrates you cared enough to do some homework on this student. Especially in a school with a large student body, treating a student like a person about whom you know something will go a long way in demonstrating that you really are concerned about the student's welfare. | |
| Address the student by name and introduce yourself (if you already know the student, remind him or her of your last encounter). Make eye contact. Thank the student for coming even if he or she is escorted by a staff member and is not there voluntarily. | Try to make a personal connection with your first sentence, especially with a student you don't know. By thanking the student for showing up, you provide a degree of respect for his or her participation in the process and allow the student to save face if he or she is there unwillingly. | "Hi, Robert. Thanks for coming. My name is Ms. Underwood and I want to chat with you for a little bit." |
| Ensure as much privacy for the contact as you can. | An effective assessment needs to ask very personal questions about a student's emotions. Under the best of circumstances, this conversation may be difficult. Making it clear you will try to provide as much confidentiality and opportunity for privacy as you can may facilitate the establishment of rapport, as well as create a safe climate for the discussion. | "Would you mind closing the door behind you? I'd like to make sure we're not interrupted." |

| What to Do | Why It Works | What to Say |
|---|---|---|
| Have a good opening statement that clarifies the purpose of the interview. | If you beat around the bush making small talk, you may confuse the student by setting a casual tone for what is a very serious conversation. Being direct about the purpose of the interview clarifies why the student is there and what you want to talk about. | "I want to talk with you today about some of your teachers' concerns about changes in your behavior and your performance in class. They've said that they're worried that something may be going on with you and wanted me to talk with you about it." |
| Directly address student's resistance if you sense it. | Although many students will be cooperative, others will not be happy about talking to you. Acknowledging a student's reluctance directly at the beginning of the interview confronts this resistance, gives you a chance to validate the student's feelings, and lets him or her know that the interview will still take place and that you appreciate even grudging cooperation. | "I can tell, Robert, that sitting here talking with me is probably the last place on earth you want to be. Talk to me about that." |
| Use simple questions. | For most students, simply being summoned to the counselor's office is an upsetting experience. And when a person is upset, emotions may cloud thinking and judgment. Add to that initial upset the distress about discussing the topic of suicide and you can understand why keeping questions open ended and simple generally leads to better responses. | "Can you tell me how long you've been feeling this way?"<br><br>"Tell me about some of the things you've done to try to deal with these feelings."<br><br>"What did you think would happen if you took those pills?" |

| What to Do | Why It Works | What to Say |
|---|---|---|
| Clarify the meanings of expressions or words. | Never assume that your definitions of words are the same as those of your students. Especially when you're asking about emotions, it is generally more helpful to ask students to explain the meaning of their word choices than to simply accept the words at face value. Their responses tend to be much more instructive and descriptive of their feelings than the words themselves.<br><br>With younger students whose feelings vocabularies are not very sophisticated, you will often hear words used out of context. That's all the more reason to ask what they mean when they use clinical words like "depressed" or "bipolar" or even more common affective expressions like "I'm bored." | "Can you tell me what you mean when you say you've felt depressed lately? The word 'depressed' can mean a lot of different things to people and I want to be sure I know what it means to you." |
| Don't presume to understand the student's feelings. | Teens in particular seem to be very put off by adults who tell them "I know how you feel." They live with the adolescent fantasy that their feelings are unique and no one, least of all an adult, could possibly understand them. As a result, they generally do not respond well to adults who insist they understand. So rather than set yourself up to be one of *those* grown-ups, admit that you don't have a clue and that you need help from them to understand what's going on with them. | "I really want to understand how you feel, which is why I'm asking you so many questions about it." |
| Summarize frequently. | The technique of summarizing what you've heard someone say is as much a tool for the speaker as it is for the listener. Stopping the flow of conversation to recap what you've heard the student say serves several purposes:<br><br>• It lets you make sure you're on the same page as the speaker.<br><br>• It helps organize the content of the conversation.<br><br>• It highlights the relevant points, which is especially useful if the student's narrative seems disjointed.<br><br>• And, simply but importantly, it shows that you have been listening carefully. | "Let me check this out—what I think I just heard you say is . . ." |

| What to Do | Why It Works | What to Say |
|---|---|---|
| Explore the personal meaning of suicide to this student. | For many people, talking about suicide or wanting to die is only the first part of the sentence. It is the "what I want to do" in response to an undefined "why." To really understand its meaning, it's essential to understand what has been going on in the student's life to precipitate the thoughts about death.<br><br>Avoid asking students what they think will happen when they die. Most school children are incapable of having anything that resembles a mature understanding of death. Questions about the afterlife will only distract both you and the student from the real issue: the problems in the student's life that have led to the thoughts of escape by suicide. | "Can you finish this sentence: I want to die because . . ." |
| Remain nonjudgmental. | It can be very difficult to keep your concern for a student's well-being out of an assessment for suicide risk. Especially if you are close to the student, it may be tempting to say that many people care about the student or that he or she has made it through hard times before. To say simply that you really want to understand why he or she wants to die so you can validate the student's distress and gather detailed information to send along with the referral can be very challenging. Remember, being nonjudgmental doesn't mean that you agree with the student's appraisal of the situation; it means that you can hear what the student says without critiquing or evaluating. | "I can only imagine the level of distress you must be feeling to be thinking about taking your life. Tell me more about it." |
| Use "joining" expressions. | Because we know that feelings of suicide can create a sense of personal isolation, a helpful interview technique is called "joining"—using words that indicate you want to connect with the student to find a better solution than suicide to the problem in his or her life. | "Based on what you've told me, I can hear your worry that the only way out of your current situation is to die. But I'd like to think if we put our heads together and involved some other resources, we could come up with a better solution that lets you stay alive." |

## LET'S REVIEW

Preparing for an assessment interview can be as important as the interview itself. In some ways, it's analogous to baking a cake: if you read the recipe first and make sure you have all the necessary ingredients, you have a better chance of making a cake that turns out well. Some of the "ingredients" for a good interview are grounded in your professional training and experience—your knowledge of developmental theory, for example, and your relationships with the faculty and staff in your school. Others require adaptation of basic interviewing techniques and the incorporation of an awareness of the risk factors and warning signs of youth suicide. Finally, one of the most essential factors for an effective risk assessment is collaboration with everyone involved in the process. With data from collaborative sources, you are well on your way to providing an assessment that will help the student get the additional resources he or she needs.

IN YOUR

# Experience . . .

- What are some of your personal techniques for helping students feel comfortable in an interview?

- Are there students with whom you have difficulty being empathetic? What challenges you about these kids?

- Think about one of the suicide assessment interviews you've done that went well. What does that tell you about your interview skills?

## HANDOUTS

5-1: Documentation of Suicide Risk
5-2: Student Assessment Interview Chart

# Chapter 6

## "Tell Me More": The Assessment Interview

*"I was so mad at myself. After this student, whom I really cared about, finished telling me that she had felt like killing herself the previous fall, I said without thinking, 'You don't still feel that way, do you?' The minute I said it, I knew I had made it almost impossible for her to tell me how she really felt now."*

—SCHOOL COUNSELOR

This counselor makes the point that it's really important to be mindful and not to be on autopilot when conducting an assessment interview with a potentially at-risk student. The last chapter laid out key steps in preparing for the interview and explained counseling techniques that can assist you in approaching the interview with intentionality—carefully thinking about and wording what you want to say. This chapter will get even more specific. It will outline what the interview should cover and provide questions that you can incorporate into the interview. It reflects the *Lifelines* "Tell Me More" approach to the interview process.

Unfortunately, for many counselors, the topic of suicide is very anxiety provoking. They may be familiar with a general line of questioning that establishes suicidal intent; however, more often than not, they leave the more in-depth questioning to the mental health professional. This is certainly appropriate, but it misses an opportunity to gather valuable information that the student may not readily share with the next person to whom he or she is referred. In addition, simply by asking the student to "tell me more" in this initial assessment, you may be able to provide your community mental health referral resource with details that support the school's observations about this student's suicide risk.

This chapter will also discuss students who may be difficult to interview and suggest intervention strategies with this population. The DVD that accompanies this manual demonstrates specific interview techniques to assist in intervention with these students who challenge our counseling skills.

By the end of this chapter, you will be able to

- understand the philosophy behind the "Tell Me More" approach
- list the topics that should be covered in an assessment interview with the student
- provide examples of specific ways to address these topics
- respond to students who make the interview process challenging

## WHAT IS THE "TELL ME MORE" APPROACH?

The "Tell Me More" approach is based on the clinical experiences of the authors in both school and community settings. It addresses the challenges school staff and other community mental health professionals face in asking youth questions about suicide.

For many of us, hearing that a youth is thinking about suicide seems like enough information; surely we don't need to know any more than that to make an appropriate referral. But when we think about the characteristics of people who are feeling suicidal, we realize that they often feel isolated in their suicidal thinking. They may be holding these thoughts as secrets that they are ashamed or embarrassed to share. By its very nature, the "Tell Me More" approach is intended to penetrate the isolation in which the suicidal person is often trapped. As we know from everyday communication, when we ask people to tell us more about what they are saying, and when we convey that we are really interested in their answers, it's easier to develop a sense of connection with them. That sense of connection is an essential ingredient in the process of helping a suicidal young person feel less alone with very scary thoughts and feelings about death, and it can be the critical first step in the help-seeking process.

For other students who may have struggled with thoughts of suicide on a chronic basis, the referral to a counselor may have become just another routine and predictable part of the process. They are familiar with the standard list of questions about suicide and often answer them even before being asked. In these situations, the "Tell Me More" approach is designed to help both the interviewer and the student think about the wish to die in different, more expansive ways. While the standard and necessary questions about suicide risk are, of course, included, they are augmented by questions or reflections that offer the student and the counselor opportunities to think about the reasons *behind* the suicidal ideation, to get a deeper and more personal understanding of what the wish to die is all about. The "Tell Me More" approach, especially in the case of students for whom thoughts of suicide are common, can be the beginning of a shift in thinking that eventually leads to other less destructive problem-solving alternatives.

## WHAT IS THE FIRST STEP IN THE "TELL ME MORE" INTERVIEW PROCESS?

Let's put this in context by using the example of an actual student referral for a suicide-risk assessment. The following information was received by a school counselor:

> This is a referral for Kate G., a seventh-grade student, by her homeroom teacher. The teacher has noticed changes in Kate's behavior over the last several months and has talked with several of her subject-area teachers who concurred that something is different about her. Previously she was a good student, but her grades have dropped. She seems not as involved with her friends and "just looks sad" according to her homeroom teacher. She was overheard in the hall telling a peer that she didn't care if she died because heaven "has got to be a better place than being here on earth."

The first step in the process addresses the questions you want to ask the school-based referral source. There may be a degree of urgency to the request to see this student and you may feel administrative pressure to do the interview as soon as possible. Even so, taking a few minutes to gather specific data that explains the reason for the referral will make it much easier to get an accurate reading of what's going on with the referred student. The following chart contains questions you might ask the teacher who referred Kate G. for an assessment. The chart also includes reasons for gathering this type of information so that you can generalize the process to other referrals.

# The Referral Source "Tell Me More"

| Questions to Ask Referral Source | Why You Are Asking |
|---|---|
| "Can you be more specific about Kate's drop in grades? What grades did she have before and what does she have now? Could the drop in grades be related to missed homework assignments or tests and quizzes?"<br><br>**Note:** While this information can be very useful, some teachers may not be prepared to be specific about grades, especially in a large school. Ask the questions, though, and get as much information as you can. Something is better than nothing. | When you talk with Kate, you will be much better prepared if you have examples to share with her rather than a generalized statement. Kate may not be aware that she seems so different, so a list of all the things her teachers have noticed may alert her to the fact that other people have seen that something has changed about her. Having this information to present in the interview also does two other things: first, it shows Kate that the teachers in the school care about her and, second, it demonstrates that you are going to ask Kate to be just as specific in providing *you* with information. The more specific she is in answering your questions, the better you will be able to understand what's been going on with her and come up with a plan to help. |
| "Which of Kate's teachers provided you with this information? Are there any classes in which her grades haven't changed?" | As you know, sometimes classroom behavior is erratic: a student may do well in several classes and poorly in others. It's important to get as complete a picture as possible of Kate's performance. If she continues to do well in some classes, you can ask her about this in the interview and reinforce that despite some changes in a negative direction, she is still doing well in other classes, which can be seen as a sign of her strength. |
| "When you say she seems not as involved with her friends, can you give me an example of what makes you say that?" | Often students who are not concerned about fluctuations in grades are worried about changes in relationships with friends. This can be especially evident in changes in the lunchroom where students will admit they are no longer sitting with the same group of peers. In addition, this question can give you clues about possible undisclosed bullying behavior, especially with elementary and middle school students (see chapter 9 for more information about bullying). Again, being able to provide Kate with the specifics of what the faculty have noticed in this area can give her permission to address the subject with you. |

| Questions to Ask Referral Source | Why You Are Asking |
|---|---|
| "Tell me what you mean when you say 'she looks sad.' How is this different from the way she seemed several months ago?" | "Sad" is a vague term. You want examples that are as specific as possible about what it means. Sometimes the best way to describe it is in contrast to previous behaviors, for example, a student who used to laugh and smile now looks on the verge of tears. |
| "Can you tell me about the circumstances of the comment Kate made about 'heaven being a better place than earth'? Who overheard Kate saying this? When did it happen and to whom was she speaking?" | Unless you know the specifics of a secondhand comment, a student can easily deny its accuracy. This comment in particular, which includes a vague reference to death, is important to explore in a risk assessment for suicide. |
| "How has Kate's attendance/tardiness been? Has she had any detentions?" | As we saw from examples in the last chapter, a change in attendance can be a concrete and observable sign that something is up with a student. Being specific about the number of absences makes a firmer statement than saying something vague like "You've been absent a lot." <br><br> Detention is another measure of behavior change. Both the number of detentions and the reasons for them can be helpful to you in supporting the school's concerns about Kate. |
| "Do you know specifically when you noticed a change in Kate?" | Knowing when Kate's behavior started to go downhill may be very helpful in trying to pinpoint a triggering event for these changes. There is another important reason for getting this information. It can remind Kate that she was functioning fine prior to these changes and that there is no reason to assume she won't function well again. |
| "Have you spoken to Kate's parents?" | If Kate's parents are already in the loop, they will be somewhat prepared for your contact with them. They may, in fact, have initiated contact with Kate's homeroom teacher because of their own concerns about her school performance. |

As you can see, taking the time to ask these questions lets you walk into the interview better prepared to talk with Kate *very specifically* about the reasons for her teachers' concerns. You will also be in a better position to talk with Kate's parents, if that seems necessary, and answer their questions about how her behavior and attitude changes seem to be affecting her school performance.

## IS THERE ANYTHING ELSE TO KEEP IN MIND DURING THE INTERVIEW WITH A STUDENT LIKE KATE?

Chapter 5 outlined strategies for preparing for the interview. There are also a couple of principles to remember while you are doing the interview:

- You can't make any bargains with Kate to keep suicidal thoughts or actions a secret or negotiate a future time to check in to give her a chance to get her act together. As you know, some students will acknowledge problems and promise to improve if you don't make a big deal out of it or contact their parents. You cannot agree to such a request.

- If you think Kate may be at risk for suicide, you cannot leave her alone! This means she will be in the room if you need to call her parents. (This will be addressed in more detail in chapter 7.)

- Be familiar with the community resources you may want to use for referral.

- Keep notes on what you say and what you do.

## ARE THERE SPECIFIC TOPICS TO COVER IN THE INTERVIEW?

Some of the main topics to cover in the interview incorporate the five characteristics of suicide introduced in chapter 2. They address the fact that (1) suicide is usually seen as an alternative to a problem the student feels can't be solved in any other way; (2) the student's thinking is in crisis mode, which interferes with problem solving; (3) there is a degree of ambivalence in the suicidal thinking; (4) the student's thinking includes irrational elements; and (5) the student is trying to communicate something to someone in his or her life through suicide.

Think of the five characteristics as the frame or scaffolding for the interview. You fill in the frame by encouraging the student to "tell me more" about what has precipitated thoughts of suicide, what those thoughts are like, and whether he or she has plans to act on them.

> ## Characteristics of Suicide
>
> 1. Suicide is viewed as an alternative to a seemingly unsolvable problem.
> 2. Crisis thinking impairs problem solving.
> 3. A suicidal person is often ambivalent.
> 4. The choice of suicide has an irrational component.
> 5. Suicide is a form of communication.

## DO SPECIFIC QUESTIONS ABOUT SUICIDE ALSO NEED TO BE INCLUDED IN THE INTERVIEW?

Absolutely. To flesh out how to incorporate the standard questions about suicide risk into an interview, let's return to our example of Kate G. By the end of the interview you should know the answers to these specific questions:

- What's going on in Kate's life that makes her feel like dying?
- Is Kate thinking about suicide now?
- How long has she been having these thoughts?
- Does she have any plans to carry out the suicide?
- Has she rehearsed the plan?
- Does she have access to the means to carry out the plan?
- Has Kate ever attempted suicide before? If so, has she told anyone? If she did, how did they react?
- Does Kate have any people in her life whom she considers to be her supports—friends, relatives, other adults?
- Despite having feelings that she wants to die, can Kate give you any reasons she has for living?
- Whom does Kate want to send a message to if she completed suicide, and what would she want that message to be?

Through the use of questions like these and incorporation of interviewing techniques that address *crisis thinking*, you effectively cover the five characteristics of suicide. For example, by asking for details about the problems in Kate's life, you can help her recognize that her consideration of suicide is an *alternative* to a problem that she feels is not solvable by any other means. You acknowledge her *ambivalence* by taking her thoughts about suicide seriously, while emphasizing that, if you put your heads together, maybe you can come up with a less destructive solution than dying. Her *irrationality* that suicide will solve all her problems is countered by your questions about any reasons she has to keep on living. Finally, the *communication* implied in the suicidal solution is directly addressed by the message she would like her suicidal intent to send.

## HOW DO I INTEGRATE ALL THIS INFORMATION INTO AN INTERVIEW?

To answer this question in a practical way, the following sections use the voices and stories of several different students whose experiences may sound familiar to you.

To start, remember that the context of an assessment interview is really no different than that of any of your other interviews or discussions with students. You want to invite the student into a safe, welcoming place, establish rapport if this is your first contact with the student, and be empathetic to the student's concerns. In the cramped offices of many schools, it may seem impossible to even consider the idea of a welcoming space. But listen to this comment from a student:

> "We used to joke that Dr. P's office looked like something out of the television series *Hoarders*—she'd have to move papers off a chair so you'd have a place to sit. But once she started to talk to you, there was something about the way she looked at you and kinda acted like you were the most important person in the world for that very second that made you forget all the stuff in the office."

Remember, it isn't the space that welcomes the student—it's you! Your genuine interest in the student talking to you and a sense that your office is a safe place makes up for the chaos that may surround you.

*Safety* often begins with the sense of being welcomed into the interview setting. Safety can be reinforced by explaining up front why the student is with you and what will be happening in your contact with him or her. It also includes what is referred to as "informed consent." This means that you are clear with the student at the beginning of the interview that if he or she says anything that makes *you* concerned about his or her personal safety, you have a legal responsibility to contact parents or guardians. It can be helpful to explain that if you feel this type of notification is necessary, you will talk with the student to collaborate on the best way to do this. Here's what that may sound like:

*Counselor:* Hi, Kate. I appreciate your coming down to talk with me. Your homeroom teacher is worried about how different you've seemed lately and that's what I want to talk with you about. I'm going to ask you some questions to see if we can put our heads together to find out what's been going on in your life. Unless I hear you talk about something that makes me worried about your personal safety, like if you're thinking about hurting or killing yourself, what we talk about stays between you and me. If I'm worried about your safety, however, I may have to contact your parents or guardians. I have a legal responsibility to do this. If that has to happen, you and I will talk about the best way for me to talk with them. How does that sound to you?

*"Jerome could not have been more annoyed when I asked him to come down to talk with me. He made it extremely clear he had nothing to say and was unresponsive to my first question. When I explained that his teachers were saying some stuff about him and I wanted to get his point of view, he opened up for the first time with a rant about what (bleep!) his teachers were. Once I got my foot in the door of conversation, I knew I could keep it open. At the end of the interview, he actually apologized for being so rude to me at the beginning of the interview."*

*—SCHOOL SOCIAL WORKER*

The next step is to *invite* the student to participate in the interview. Engaging the student in the helping process is, in truth, a formality. Most students know you're going to ask them questions whether they agree to the process or not. Yet the invitation, framed as simply as the statement "I want to ask you a bit more about what's going on," demonstrates your desire to respect the student and sets the stage for your asking what might feel like intrusive questions. Students can and may respond affirmatively ("Sure"), neutrally ("Whatever"), or negatively ("I have nothing to say"). In the last case, simply validate their feelings ("I appreciate that this may seem like a waste of time to you") and then explain that the school has expressed some concerns about what's been going on with him or her lately that you need to talk about.

## WHAT COMES NEXT?

Here's an outline for the "Tell Me More" questions about suicide risk:

Explore concerns about risk in a logical sequence. First, list the reasons for your concerns.

> *Counselor:* Kate, your homeroom teacher has expressed some concerns about your performance lately. She said your grades have really fallen. She also said you don't seem as involved with your friends. She told me you've been seen skipping lunch several days a week to go to the library. More than that, she told me you just seem sad— she said you seem on the verge of tears quite often. You're also missing school a lot—seven times in the last four weeks. Please *tell me more* about what's going on.

Be patient with the student's response. Expect to hear "It's nothing" or "I don't know." Continue to explore concerns related to school until the student acknowledges a shift in behavior and/or attitude.

> *Kate:* Yeah, I guess my teachers are right. I've been having some stuff going on during this semester and I can't concentrate so much on my schoolwork.

This kind of remark provides an opening to ask more about what's going on in the student's life that may be the trigger for the behavior changes. Try to use the student's own words (unless they happen to be expletives and then substitute something with a similar meaning).

> *Counselor: Tell me more* about what some of the "stuff" has been.

It's hard to know what kind of response you'll get to this request. You may get a litany of what the student feels are disasters ("My parents are getting divorced, my boyfriend's parents found out we're having sex, and my so-called friends have been spreading rumors about me on Facebook"); a single event that feels like a disaster, even to you ("Ever since my cousin took his life last summer, I haven't been myself"); or an honest "I have no idea—all I know is I feel miserable."

Whether the response includes a single event or a long list of accumulated problems, use the interview techniques of clarifying and summarizing to verify that you have an accurate understanding of what the student's been telling you.

*Counselor:* So what I think I heard you tell me is that the death of your grandmother has turned your life upside down. You've been feeling pretty miserable, so you've been skipping school and you've gotten yourself into a pretty tough drinking crowd of older kids. At first you liked all your new friends. But now they kind of scare you and you are feeling like your life is getting out of control fast. You're really afraid you might do something bad. Did I get that right?

*"The counselor asked me if I thought about hurting myself and I said 'no.' When she found out later I wanted to die, she asked me why I hadn't been truthful with her. I told her that I had been very truthful—I didn't want to just hurt myself, I wanted to kill myself. 'Oh,' she said, 'oh.'"*

—ELEVEN-YEAR-OLD BOY

Ask directly about suicide. It's important to frame this question clearly. Asking students if they have thought of hurting themselves is not the same as asking if they have thought of killing themselves. You can be very direct: "Are you thinking about suicide?" You can also phrase the question in a more indirect manner:

- "I know you said heaven had to be a better place than being here on earth. Are you thinking about taking your life?"

- "You know, when people have so many things falling apart in their lives, they sometimes feel like life isn't worth it anymore. Have you been having these feelings?"

Whether you ask the question directly or indirectly, always be prepared to follow up with a sequence of questions about suicide itself:

"*Tell me more* about what kinds of thoughts you're having about dying."

You are asking the student to explain the details of the suicidal thoughts. For some students, the thoughts may simply be thoughts that are not attached to lethal courses of action.

*Counselor:* Tell me, Kate, when you think about suicide, what do you think you would do?

> *Kate:* I just think I'd rather be dead. I don't think about a way
> to do it.

For other students, the thinking may have gone much further and be much more specific.

> *Adam:* I think about hanging myself in my closet with one of
> my neckties or a belt. Yes, I think a belt would work
> better because it's stronger.

Obviously, the risk for suicide may be higher with a student like Adam who has a specific, well-thought-out plan. In this case, the information you have gathered leads you to believe that the student is at imminent risk and that the suicide might take place at any time. This situation is definitely beyond the purview of the school and should include an immediate phone call to parents with a referral to an off-campus mental health resource for further assessment and evaluation.

While some students may admit to plans that could be carried out with any number of easily accessible items, especially if they are considering hanging as a method, the plans of other students may rely on access to means. "Means" can include pills, drugs, and guns or other weapons. As we saw in chapter 4, access to means is a serious risk factor for suicide. It is important to evaluate access to determine the immediacy of a referral. The question about access to means can be put simply and directly:

> "Do you have access to the pills (or the gun, etc.) right now, or do
> you know where and how to get them?"

If you discover in your interview that the student has access to means, ask those "Tell Me More" follow-up questions that give more clarity about the exact nature of the accessible means. These can include questions like the following:

- "How many pills do you have? What kind of pills are they? Where did you get them? Can you get access to more? Does anybody know you have them?"

- "Where can you get a gun? Have you ever used a gun before? Do you have ammunition? Does anybody know you have a gun?"

Obviously, this will be *essential* information to pass along to both the student's parents and to the person or agency to which you are making a referral. For strategies for talking with parents about access to means, refer to chapter 7, page 125.

The risk will also be higher for a student who has made a previous attempt (see chapter 7 for more information about previous attempts). Asking about previous attempts often gets overlooked when there is concern about imminent risk, but the question should be included in your tool kit of questions, as it provides valuable information about the student's view of suicide as a coping strategy.

> *Counselor:* I hear you telling me, Adam, that right now you've got a pretty serious plan. I'm wondering if you've made similar plans in the past or have even made a suicide attempt.
>
> *Adam:* Well, actually, I did make an attempt last summer. That's how I know the necktie might not be strong enough.

The next area of questioning involves the frequency of the thoughts (although with a student like Adam you already have enough information to make an immediate referral).

> *Counselor:* How often do you have these thoughts, Adam?
>
> *Adam:* Pretty often.
>
> *Counselor:* Help me understand better how much that means. Once a week, once a day, more than that?
>
> *Adam:* At least once a day.

As you can see, it can be helpful to provide examples of time frames when students give vague answers to this question. A student who is having frequent thoughts may not even be aware of how often they are occurring or may be embarrassed to admit how frequently they occur. By providing these time frames, you may help the student realize how often the thoughts and feelings are occurring. You may also give the reluctant student permission to acknowledge how intrusive and frequent the thoughts might really be. It can be helpful to ascertain whether the thoughts are more frequent at certain times of the day, such as in the evening or during school. Thoughts about death may be interfering with the student's sleep, for example, or compromising his or her ability to concentrate in school.

> *Counselor:* Do these thoughts come more often at certain times of the day or night?
>
> *Adam:* Mostly at home, at night, when the house is really quiet. That's when I think about dying.

In addition to these questions, however, you will want to ask "Have you told anyone else of your plans?"

Many students will admit that they have confided their plans to a peer. If this young person who had been told about the planned suicide also attends your school, you may consider exploring his or her reactions to being the recipient of this disclosure. It may also be helpful to remind this student how critical it is to take even what seem insignificant threats seriously and to talk to a trusted adult about them.

*"I knew Max told several of his old girlfriends that he was planning on killing himself way before he did it. None of them took it seriously. Maybe if they had, he'd still be here today."*

—EIGHTH-GRADE BOY

Sometimes, there may be multiple threats that peers either don't take seriously or don't know how to handle, so they do nothing. Listen to what one of the girls to whom Max confided his suicidal thoughts had to say:

*"I thought Max was okay because he went into counseling and I was sure he must be telling his counselor how much he wanted to die. I did think about telling my mom, but I didn't think there was anything she could do. When I got the phone call that Max had jumped off the roof, I wanted to die myself."*

—FRESHMAN GIRL

Questions about the meaning or the intent of the suicide are also very instructive. They address the characteristic of suicide as some type of communication and often provide additional helpful information for the student's subsequent mental health treatment.

**Counselor:** Becca, tell me more about who you wanted to send a message to with your suicide attempt.

**Becca:** I don't know. The girls who keep saying mean things about me, I guess.

**Counselor:** And what did you want that message to be?

**Becca:** That it's all their fault for being so mean to me. And I hope they feel terrible.

The last area you may want to explore is whether the student sees any deterrents or has any protective factors for suicide (see chapter 10 for more information on protective factors). There are a couple of ways to ask this question. The first is to ask what could change in the student's life to make him or her feel that there is no need to resort to suicide. Here, for example, is Becca's response:

> *Becca:* Well, if those girls would just leave me alone and not keep picking on me and trying to start fights when no one is looking, and if someone would just believe me when I tell them how bad it really is, that would make a difference.

The second approach is helping a desperate student to focus on reasons for living. This does not diminish or discount the suicidal intent; it merely shifts the focus to what may be the student's small, remaining investments in living.

> *Counselor:* Tell me about anything, Becca, that you feel you have to live for?

> *Becca:* Nothing . . . well, maybe my dog. That's it. My dog.

### Another Interesting Question

People who are feeling suicidal lose the ability to use fantasy in productive ways. An interesting question to pose to a suicidal student is "If you could be anywhere in the world right now, doing anything you want to do, rather than sitting here talking to me, where would you be and what would you be doing?" If a student can give an imaginative answer (for example, home playing the guitar, hanging out with my friends, playing a video game), you sense that this student still has a bit of coping intact. If a student replies, "I'd rather be dead," you have another clear warning sign of suicide risk.

## TO REVIEW, WHAT ARE THE AREAS OF QUESTIONING TO INCLUDE IN THE "TELL ME MORE" ASSESSMENT INTERVIEW?

### *"Tell Me More" Assessment Interview Outline*

- List specific reasons for your concerns.
- Address suicide directly:
  - "Tell me what kinds of thoughts you've been having about dying."
  - "How often do you have them?"
  - "How specific are they?"

    "Do you have a plan?"

    "Have you rehearsed?"

    "Do you have access to a way to carry out your plan?"
  - "Have you told anybody about your thoughts or plan?"
  - "Have you ever made a suicide attempt before?"
  - "If something could change about your life to make you not feel suicidal, what would that be?"
  - "Tell me any reasons you have to keep living."
  - "What message do you want to send with your suicidal intentions?" "To whom do you want to send that message?"

## HOW DO I INTERVIEW A STUDENT WHO IS REALLY DIFFICULT?

The place to start is to examine why the student seems so difficult. Most of the time, the difficulty belongs to us—our interviewing skills are challenged by the student's personality, attitude, situation—take your pick! If we can change our use of the word "difficult" to "challenging," we take ownership of the problem and, as you know from your basic training as a counselor, any problem you personally own is an easier problem to fix.

The following chart includes reasons students may be challenging and some suggested strategies for responding to them.

| Student Type | Suggested Intervention Strategies |
|---|---|
| **Unresponsive/ monosyllabic** | Ask direct questions that are open ended. Ask for clarification, more details, so you can better understand. ("Can you give me some examples that might help me understand a little better?") |
| **Monopolizer** | Some students answer questions with paragraphs or even pages. Make frequent summaries and redirect. Don't pursue irrelevant details. Be active in setting the structure and limits of the interview. ("I know you have a lot more you could say about that, but I'd like to move us along so we can cover all the important information.") |
| **Joker/flippant** | Ignore as much as you can; then confront. ("We're talking about some pretty difficult topics right now and you keep making jokes. I'm confused—does this seem funny to you?")<br><br>Interpret. ("People often make jokes about topics they find difficult.") |
| **Angry** | Acknowledge the feelings. Let the student vent. Validate feelings. ("I can see you're pretty angry about having to talk with me. Tell me about it.") Remind the student of your role. ("My job in the school is to talk with students who seem to be having difficulties.") |
| **Tearful** | Have tissues available. Be directive. Let the student cry for a while, but then keep the interview moving. If you just sit quietly for a long period of time, your silence may encourage the student to avoid talking and just keep crying. |
| **Agitated** | Try interjecting deep breathing techniques into the interview. Let the student know that using these techniques can help with anxieties and worries. |
| **"Frequent Flyer"** | Empathize with the student's frequent distress. Reinforce the importance of problem-solving a better and more lasting solution than suicide threats to deal with problems. Collaborate with the community resource to explain the frequency of the student's suicidal threats and the need to try to find better problem-solving options. |
| **Unlikeable** | Own YOUR feelings! Try to see past your personal dislike of the student to the underlying pain or distress. |
| **Cultural minority** | Ask the student to explain the cultural context of specific behaviors. Remember that despite cultural differences, the underlying feelings are always the same. |
| **Untruthful** | Do your homework. Approach the interview with indisputable facts. ("You've missed two weeks of school; your grades have dropped. You are missing ten homework assignments in chemistry.") You don't have to accuse the student of lying if you stick to what you know. ("Despite the fact that you see the facts differently than I do, the bottom line is that we're concerned about your behavior.") |

Because it may be helpful to see some of these suggested strategies demonstrated, you can find several interview segments with challenging students on the *Lifelines Intervention* DVD.

A word of caution: not every student who is referred to you will be at risk for suicide. For some students, threats of suicide represent cries of frustration or attempts to get school or parental attention. Be careful not to assume that every student who talks about wanting to die is really at risk for suicide. Especially with younger students who have very limited vocabularies for expressing feelings, saying "I want to die" may be a shorthand expression for feeling helpless, desperate, or trapped. It can also be used to gain power in a family when a child knows it will stop everybody in their tracks and deflect attention from the problem or situation the child is having trouble handling.

If you ask about suicide and a student minimizes the threat ("I say that all the time when I'm fed up with things") or denies its importance ("I didn't really mean it"), acknowledge the student's feelings but continue with the interview, paying attention to the other verbal and nonverbal cues the student is sending. You may determine at the end of the interview that the student is being honest when he or she denies suicidal intent, or you may need a second opinion to assess the intentionality of the student's remarks. Or you may be in a school district where even

## Sam

Sam was a fifth-grade student who generally kept beneath school radar. In his after-school program, however, he was a real challenge, getting into fights with other students, ignoring program rules, breaking into tears when chastised by staff over any of his infractions. His mother reported that he would often cry at night that he hated after-school care and if he had to go back he would "rather die." She took Sam to a counselor who determined that Sam's threats represented his extreme displeasure at being in the after-school program. After they discussed alternatives, the threats stopped. A year later, however, Sam was back at the counselor's office having threatened suicide again after a fight with his mother. After some questioning, Sam admitted he had wanted to upset his mother so he said he wanted to die. He didn't mean it in the slightest, he said, but knew it was the best way to get back at his mom. The counselor and Sam discussed better ways for Sam to deal with his anger and, after three years, he has not threatened suicide again.

casual threats of suicide ("I can't stand all these tests—I think I'll shoot myself") require outside intervention. With students like these, your intervention can be directed at helping them use a less self-destructive way to communicate their frustration, anger, or disappointment. These are the students who may be helped by the curriculum in *Lifelines: A Suicide Prevention Program* that teaches students help-seeking skills for themselves and others.

## LET'S REVIEW

Building on the information covered in the previous chapters, this chapter detailed the areas of questioning to cover in the "Tell Me More" assessment. It not only reviewed precise areas of questioning but also sequenced them in a way that makes it easier for both you and the student to follow. By the end of this phase of the assessment, you should have gathered enough information to be very clear about your reasons for community referral for additional assessment. The next part of the process, which is covered in the following chapters, addresses the strategic approach to the referral itself.

## IN YOUR
# Experience . . .

- As you read the questions to ask and the topics to cover, which of them were new to you?
- Have you ever dealt with a student who had access to immediate means? How did you handle the situation?
- What student behaviors do you find most challenging? What techniques have you developed to deal with them?

# Chapter 7

# Engaging Parents

*"When we got the call from the school that we needed to come to a meeting to talk about our son's possible risk for suicide, I've got to be honest, we were shocked and terrified. We felt like failures as parents that we hadn't picked up on this ourselves! I can't even put into words how helpful and comforting the counselor was. He was very clear about why the school was concerned, he explained what our options were, and he had talked Joey into going for an evaluation at the local mental health center. Maybe even more, he didn't make us feel bad as parents. As a matter of a fact, he made us feel good because we were going to get help for Joey as soon as we left."*

—MOTHER OF TWELVE-YEAR-OLD BOY

Parents are an essential part of the competent youth suicide prevention community. School staff can be trained and well prepared to identify students who may be at risk for suicide, and school resource team members can be effective in completing initial assessments that justify the school's concerns. However, it falls to parents and/or guardians to accomplish the next step in the process. Without parent understanding and cooperation, the referral for additional evaluation or mental health treatment may not take place.

Yet what most educators acknowledge is that it seems increasingly difficult to engage parents in school-related programs, activities, or even child-centered concerns. Part of this difficulty may certainly be related to the myriad pressures parents feel in an increasingly demanding world.

Most experts agree—the world has become a different and more complex place since the advent of the technological revolution. In fits and starts since the 1950s—when the term "stress" was primarily used to describe the physical pressure exerted on structures like buildings and bridges—personal stress management has grown to be a $9.4 billion industry. From personal experience, we can all testify to the fact that the world is indeed a different place, and so are the families that inhabit it. No family is immune to the stress and pressure common in the twenty-first century.

How do these changes affect the ability of families to respond to the needs of a potentially suicidal child? This chapter will address this question as well as provide guidelines for engaging the parents of today's children in the helping process.

Parents are such an important part of the process, yet school counselors have very little guidance to help them engage reluctant or resistant parents in the intervention process. This chapter will provide basic information about families to put the parental role into context. It will outline reasons for what is often perceived by counselors as lack of parental cooperation. Finally, it will present strategies for developing a good working relationship with parents.

By the end of this chapter, you will be able to

- recognize how the world of the twenty-first century affects youth and families

- list steps for preparing to meet with parents/guardians of a potentially suicidal child

- identify parental reactions to having a suicidal child

- outline reasons for parental resistance to getting involved in the helping process and identify response strategies

- understand how to structure a parental contact

- answer common questions about the use of mental health resources

## HOW IS THE WORLD DIFFERENT FOR YOUTH GROWING UP TODAY?

The answer to this question must start with the premise that the world is different for *each* generation of students. These differences or changes are rarely recognized by the students themselves but are generally most pronounced to the older adults in their lives who are keenly aware that "things were different in our day."

Through the eyes of most students, the world today is a technological and fast-paced place. A so-called culture of violence is played out in video games and media and echoed in the angry street slang that has become commonplace language.

> ### From "Whore to a Chainsaw" by Thy Art Is Murder
>
> You maggots
> Swarm my earth
> Infect me with putrid disease
> Your vermin
> Your genocide
> Extermination, extermination of whores
>
> I take a chainsaw to my ultimate despise
> Whore to a chainsaw is my purist form of pride
>
> I cannot live with them amongst this mess
> Amongst this mess
> I need to end this
> Insult to the human population of this world . . .

Music and music videos advocate the use of drugs and alcohol and contain explicit lyrics that present and encourage suicide as a solution to problems. There is, it would seem, a level of hostility that was not quite as blatant in students—or their schools—even ten years ago.

Coupled with edgy language is the informality of a communication system that has its roots in cyberspace. With lightning speed, kids can text thoughts and feelings that they would often not have the courage to say in person, creating wounds in peer relationships that are sometimes impossible to heal. Bullying, which has always been an unfortunate dimension of childhood and adolescence, has been taken up a notch with often anonymous and untraceable cyber-messages on social networking sites. Parents are warned about "Internet predators," who may stalk their children disguised as peers, or about the ease with which unsupervised children can access Internet pornography sites.

At an even more dramatic level, the climate of life as members of other generations knew it was forever changed by the events of September 11th, 2001. While the last decade of the twentieth century held harbingers of terrorism in the 1993 bombing of the World Trade Center and the 1995 bombing in Oklahoma City, the tragedy of 9/11 ushered in visible changes in security and postings of terror alerts and in the unnerving recognition that the United States is no longer protected by its oceans or its borders with friendly countries.

Not only has life in the larger global community become more dangerous and unpredictable; school is no longer the haven of safety it was prior to the events of

April 20, 1999. The Columbine incident in Littleton, Colorado, followed by a spate of school shootings across the county, altered parents' perception that they could send their children safely to school every morning.

Into this chaotic ecosystem, put children and teens who are often challenged by simply getting up on time in the morning and making it through a day at school. With physical maturity that generally exceeds their emotional capacity, they are faced with the same developmental tasks that have confronted the generations that preceded them: figuring out who they are, what's important to them, and what they want to do with their lives. While these tasks are always colored by the current state of the world in which adolescents live, the contemporary fast-paced climate, with its underpinnings of fear about personal safety, presents several unique elements to the children growing up today.

*"First time we took a plane trip after September 11th, my kids were totally freaked out by the soldiers and police officers they saw with guns all over the airport. We don't travel that much, so it was pretty upsetting for me as their mom, too, but I tried to explain it was for our safety. Then my son came to me a while later and asked me about this 'shoe bomber' and all I could tell him was some people are not very nice. To be honest, I'm the one who's scared of flying now."*

—MOTHER

In addition, we can't forget the normal range of stressful life events that affect students and their families: death, divorce, moving, illness, financial pressures, and so on. It's an exhausting list!

Remember, though, that the news is not all bad. Some of the same aspects of today's life and culture that create speed bumps for kids can also open the doors to opportunity. The capacity for instant connection afforded by the Internet, for example, can put kids in touch with a world they could only begin to imagine. Video gaming teaches them the dexterity, cleverness, and proficiency that can be essential in a technologically driven world. Digital communication skills may be different from more personalized communication techniques; however, they can also prepare students to become participating citizens in the evolving world of cyberspace.

The trick for adults with varying degrees of responsibility for this generation of children is to remain open minded about both the blessings and the curses of the modern world. When you are reaching out and trying to engage parents, in particular, try to be empathetic to their more global worries for their children. Recognize that stress and pressure come from many directions and that the sense of frustration and helplessness parents bring to your office may be about a variety of other major concerns that have nothing to do with their children. In your interview with parents, try to bring an understanding of the challenges of growing up in the world today as well as an appreciation of its opportunities; seek to approach parents from a realistic, shared, and informed perspective.

## HOW CAN I APPLY THIS INFORMATION TO TALKING WITH PARENTS WHO MIGHT HAVE A CHILD AT RISK FOR SUICIDE?

Not all of the parents you see will have a keen appreciation for every aspect of the social culture as it affects either themselves or their child. Nevertheless, there's a good chance that some element of the social context is having an impact on their family. Listen to how a high school social worker explains it:

> "Over the course of a week, I was amazed at how often the students or parents I interacted with referred to larger social issues in connection with the problems the student was having in school. For example, Laurel T. had recently been approached by someone who was determined to be an Internet predator and the local police were involved; Ryan K. was being bullied on an anonymous website called FormSpring, where someone had written he should 'do the world a favor and die'; the parents of Ming L. and Rob T. had just lost their jobs in downsizing; and Maura H., who had a friend who had recently died by suicide, just learned her parents are getting divorced."

Although your primary point of reference is the school, for the students and families you see, a bigger picture often competes for the family's attention and resources. Simply keep this in the back of your mind. It's not necessary to get all the details about this bigger picture—the pressures the family and student feel outside the school. It's enough for you to know there *are* pressures and stresses that may be partly responsible for the behavior the student is exhibiting at school.

If you are making a referral for an at-risk student who seems to be dealing with external pressures, encourage that student and his or her parents to be forthcoming about what's going on in the family's life with the person to whom you are referring them. You'd be surprised how often families fail to make connections between stresses in the family and changes in a student's performance or behavior at school.

> ## Remember the Big Picture!
>
> "You'd have thought I would have connected the dots, but since my husband and I had been separated for almost a year, I just didn't think that the fact that we were finally getting a divorce would affect the kids. Tommy in particular seemed pretty sad, but until the counselor called me into school to talk about how his grades had dropped so badly, I didn't even think about it."
>
> —*Mother of Seventh-grade Boy*

## ARE THERE WAYS TO PREPARE TO TALK WITH PARENTS?

It's always helpful to be proactive rather than reactive. When meeting with parents or guardians, make sure to do your homework before they arrive. The more clear, observable, and concrete information you can provide them about the reasons for the school's concerns, the less you have to defend what may sound like an arbitrary position. Although you may not have to prove your case, as it were, it can be helpful to provide as much evidence as you can to validate your reasons for referring parents to the services you're recommending.

Based on our experience, here are some general tips and guidelines that might help you prepare for an interaction with parents.

### 1. Engage students in the process of involving and approaching parents.

Start by asking the student to predict his or her parents' reactions to being asked to come in to talk with you. More often than not, the student will have an accurate picture of how they will react and what they will have to say. Knowing what to expect, even before you make the phone call, can help you plan ways to deal with possible parental resistance. It can also be validating and reassuring to a student to know you are taking his or her observations into account as you decide how to approach the parents.

*"When Ms. P asked me to give her some tips on calling my parents, I thought she was kidding. But when I realized she really meant it, I told her my dad would be easier to talk to than my mom and I gave her some suggestions about what might make him listen to her. So when she called my dad and did what I had just told her, I was like, hey, she listened!"*

—*EIGHTH-GRADE BOY*

> ### Tips for Preparing to Meet Parents
>
> - Get input from the student
> - Assume parents want the best for their kids
> - Stay calm and nonjudgmental
> - Expect anger, shock, and denial
> - Don't take parents' anger personally
> - Anticipate previous experience with the mental health system
> - Avoid power struggles

## 2. Assume that all parents want to act in the best interest of their children.

If you can hold on to this belief, you may be less inclined to respond negatively to parents whose behavior may be very off-putting. As one seasoned school psychologist explained:

> "I try hard to remember that underneath it all, parents who yell, swear, and accuse me or the school of conspiring to ruin the life of their child by suggesting a mental health evaluation are simply afraid of the implication that maybe they, as parents, have failed. Or they may also be intimidated by the mental health system or ignorant of the ways counseling can help. I *try* to remember this when a parent is yelling at me. I'm better at it than I used to be!"

## 3. Remain nonjudgmental and calm, especially in the face of anger or personal accusations.

Just as there are students who can push your buttons, there will also be parents whose approach to the problems of their children is hard for you to understand. When that happens, take a deep breath and stay cool. Remember those basic interviewing skills you learned in your professional training, especially to maintain a steady, even pace of conversation if the other person is escalating in tone and volume. Don't interrupt or try to change the subject if you are confronted with an angry parent. Acknowledge the anger and try not to take it personally.

> *Counselor:* I can see, Mr. X, that you're pretty angry about having been called here to this meeting.
>
> *Mr. X:* Angry doesn't even begin to touch it. Who do you think you are, making some judgment about my child's

mental health? You are a school counselor, not a psychiatrist. How dare you!

*Counselor:* I can understand why you might see it that way.

When you encounter a parent like Mr. X, who seems to perceive the school's concern as a personal assault at the same time he is impugning your skills as a counselor, it's important to have the supporting documentation from other teachers and from school records to illustrate that you are simply the messenger who is relaying the concerns of school faculty and administration. This helps take the focus off you and places it back on the student, where it belongs.

> *Counselor:* Actually, Mr. X, I've got some documentation here from several of your son's teachers that demonstrates a sharp decline in his performance. I've also got some class work that suggests that he has been preoccupied with themes of death and suicide.

Sometimes, though, you will be extremely concerned about the student. You may have a personal connection to that student, for example, or the evidence about possible suicide risk may be so strong that your professional responsibility indicates that you must be adamant about the need for immediate additional assessment.

> *Counselor:* While I'm not a psychiatrist, Mr. X, I do have considerable experience dealing with youth. I'm basing my concerns for your son on both my experience and the evidence we have observed. These lead me to believe James may be at a high degree of risk for suicide.
>
> *or*
>
> *Counselor:* Unfortunately, Mr. X, I have known too many parents who felt the way you do and missed the opportunity to get help for their children. You are certainly within your rights to question our assessment at the school, which is why we require that you take James to be evaluated by a mental health professional.

## 4. Be prepared for parents to react with shock and denial.

Even when you have documentation, it may take a while for what you are telling the parents to sink in, especially if they have been unaware of anything different with their child. There is a grave enormity to what you are communicating to parents—that their child may want to die—and it can take a while for that realization to settle. In fact, the shock and denial may still be present during the subsequent assessment by an off-campus mental health professional. Your job is *not* to make the shock disappear; it's simply to empower parents to act in spite of it!

> *Counselor:* I know what I'm saying may be a bit difficult to accept. That's why I'm making a recommendation for you to see a mental health professional who will provide a more comprehensive evaluation than we're able to do at the school. This person will be able to answer your questions and work with you on a plan to help your son feel better.

## 5. Expect that some parents will have had previous experiences with the mental health system.

Some parents will already have experience with the mental health system, some of which may have been good and some of which may have been not so good. If their previous experiences were perceived as helpful, it will obviously be a lot easier to get the parents to accept this current referral. With negative experiences, however, you will probably have a harder sell. In these situations, validate parental experiences by acknowledging that, unfortunately, not all professionals are as helpful as others. Emphasize that you are going to do your best to make a referral that meets their child's needs. Avoid getting into a discussion that leads to "bashing" a particular agency or mental health organization. As you know, there are always two sides to every story, and you don't need to take one side against the other. Your job is simply to acknowledge that the parent had a less than satisfactory experience and to try to provide a referral that better meets the family's needs. Sometimes, however, in a community with limited mental health resources, you may have no choice but to send the parents back to a place they felt was unhelpful. In these cases, it might be useful to offer to call the community referral resource to iron out the differences and alert the agency to the parents' return for additional services. Especially when the referral is precipitated by concern for a suicidal child, it may be necessary to address issues that caused the previous problems between the agency and the family. For example, if the family's displeasure is related to having been seen by someone they perceived to be an inexperienced counselor, a more senior staff member might be assigned to the family for this referral.

## 6. Avoid power struggles with parents.

When their child is actively thinking about dying, sometimes the only semblance of control that remains for parents is to insist that they still know what's best for their child. You don't have to take this away from them by pointing out that the child's problems may suggest otherwise. You can simply emphasize the school's policies and procedures that require mental health clearance when there is even the suspicion that a student may be at risk for suicide. Validate that they do know what's best and when they get information from the evaluation, you are sure they will make the right decisions about their child's well-being and safety.

> *Counselor:* I understand you feel that the school is overreacting to what your son said about wishing he were dead. I hope you can understand, however, that our school policy requires that anytime a student says anything about being dead or dying, we require an evaluation by a mental health professional outside the school. I appreciate your cooperation with our school's rules.

## WHAT DO I SAY WHEN I PHONE THE PARENTS TO COME IN FOR A MEETING?

### The Story of Camille

"I had seen Camille in school-based counseling a few times. She had dropped a few hints about having a problem she could not share with me or with anyone. This day she came in looking especially agitated and distressed. At first she was very unresponsive. But gradually she started to tell me how upset she had been, and how her parents hadn't even noticed. When the bell rang at the end of the period, she got up and started to leave. With her hand on the doorknob, she turned to me and said, 'You know, you're the only reason I'm still alive.'

"Of course I had her sit down again with me, and then she started to cry. She told me that she had been so depressed that she couldn't focus on schoolwork at all. Several teachers had sent home warning notices because her grades, previously stellar, were falling badly. Camille's parents had grounded her because of her grades, so all she was doing now was sitting in her room and crying. The marking period was almost over, which meant that Camille's next report card was due soon. She was 'petrified' of how furious her parents were going to be. Upon further questioning about her doorknob comment, she admitted that she had been thinking a lot lately that she would

*The Story of Camille continued on next page*

**The Story of Camille** (continued)

be better off dead and that she had been considering taking a bottle of Tylenol to get her 'out of this mess.'

"I reminded Camille that, when a student tells me something like that, I really needed to tell the parents. She got even more upset, sobbing that her parents 'would be so angry' at her. Trying to calm and support her, I assured her that I would do my best to explain to them how sad and hopeless she had been feeling and that she really needed some help. I also promised her that she could stay in the room with me while I called her parents, so that she would know exactly what I said.

"When I called Camille's home (with Camille sitting tearfully on the couch next to me), I told Mrs. J that Camille was very depressed and upset and that I really felt that she needed some help right away. I asked her mother if she could come to the school to meet with me and her daughter. At first Mrs. J dismissed my concerns and seemed rather annoyed. She suggested that Camille was a 'drama queen' who 'just wanted attention.' However, when I told her that Camille had even been thinking that she would be better off dead and that she had been considering taking a bottle of Tylenol, Mrs. J replied that she would call her husband and that they would be at the school in an hour."

—*School Psychologist*

The story of Camille illustrates how prepared school resource staff need to be when calling parents to inform them about their child's potential suicide risk. This psychologist moved quickly from plan A, presenting general concerns to Camille's parents, to plan B, outlining the specifics of Camille's plans for self-harm.

With this example in mind, here are suggestions for calling parents to inform them of the school's concerns that their child might be at risk for suicide:

1. Begin by telling the student that you need to call his or her parents because you are concerned about his or her safety and because you are required to let parents know when their child may be in danger.

2. Ask for the student's input about what to expect during the phone call.

3. Explain to the student what you are going to say to the parents, and keep the student in the room with you while you make the call.

4. When you call the parents, summarize your concerns briefly and ask the parents to meet with you and the student at the school.

5. If the parents seem reluctant to come in, provide a little more detail.

6. If necessary, state that school policy requires parents to come to the school to meet with a counselor when their child has made a statement regarding possible suicide. If the parents are not able to come to the school immediately, remember that the safety of the student is paramount. Don't release the student back to class or let him or her sit alone without supervision by an adult.

## HOW DO PARENTS REACT TO BEING TOLD THAT THEIR CHILD IS SUICIDAL?

When children enter preschool or elementary school, parents begin to get regular feedback from relative strangers about their children. Everyone hopes the feedback will be positive, but parents rarely exit their child's school career without a message or two about something troubling: a low grade, an altercation with a friend, a problem on the school bus. Most families, just like most individuals, initially try to work out these problems for themselves. They might seek advice from other family members, friends, maybe even neighbors, but problem solving usually occurs close to home.

This holds true even with a problem as serious as a potentially suicidal child. In a crisis like suicide, many families "circle the wagons," conferring with trusted, close resources to figure out what, if anything, to do about this disturbing concern. When the school inserts itself into the mix, as most school policies require, families are forced to expose what may feel like a very private issue to the scrutiny and questions of total strangers.

Combine this with the innate human tendency for parents to feel responsible for their children's functioning. Just as we feel a sense of pride in our children's accomplishments, we feel a sense of responsibility for their problems. That sense of responsibility may be especially keen when parents are told that their child might be suicidal.

What are other ways parents might react? Read the following chart and compare it to your own experiences. This chart is also found on the CD-ROM.

7-1

# Common Reactions from Parents Who Have Been Informed That Their Child Is Suicidal

| Parental Reaction | Explanation | How to Address It |
|---|---|---|
| 1. Denial— "Not my kid." | The denial can be the result of a variety of factors. Many parents, for example, have no idea that suicide is the third-leading cause of death in adolescence. Their denial of the problem in this situation may be the result of being uninformed. | Explain that suicide *is* a very significant possibility. Too many parents have felt this way and missed opportunities to get help for their children before it was too late. Refer them to www.sptsusa.org and encourage them to view the *"Not My Kid"* video that addresses common parental questions about teen suicide. |
| 2. Shock and defensiveness— "You don't know what you're talking about." | This type of reaction can reflect fear of being labeled a bad parent. "If I had been a better parent, this never would have happened" is the unspoken message from these parents. | Validate the parents' feelings: "I can understand this seems to be coming out of the blue." Remind them that suicide is an unfortunate reality for today's kids. You want to try to help them understand that there are a lot of kids who struggle with suicide and that their child is one of them. Emphasize how good it was to identify what was going on before something really serious happened. |
| 3. Self-blame | This reaction reflects an element of embarrassment and personal failure. "I'm a bad parent because my son is suicidal." | Assure parents that there is no one to blame when a child is feeling suicidal. Speak to how common thoughts of suicide are for youth today. Remind the parents that suicide is related to a problem the youth is struggling to solve through a very destructive means. Thank the parents for showing their concern by their willingness to meet with you and follow your recommendations. |
| 4. Feeling overwhelmed | Especially for families that have been addressing other pressures, hearing that their child might be suicidal may be the proverbial straw that breaks the camel's back—"This is just too much— we are already at the breaking point— this will push us over the edge." | Validate feelings. Remind the parents that you are now involved with them to help them deal with this crisis with their child and that you will do everything you can to try to help them address the problem. |

| Parental Reaction | Explanation | How to Address It |
|---|---|---|
| 5. Immobilized | Some families are already so limited—one or both parents might be depressed or they may have been trying unsuccessfully to cope with a difficult child for some time. Whatever the reason—the family resources are depleted and the parents are simply empty—"We've already tried everything—there's nothing left to do." | Empathize with the family's situation, and let the parents know you will do everything you can to get the appropriate resources to help them deal with their child's distress. Don't minimize what they've been through—just remind them you're there with them now to try to move toward a better outcome. |
| 6. Angry | These parents may express anger at their child for even thinking about suicide. Or if the child has expressed suicidal thoughts in the past, they may be annoyed that the "problem" wasn't "fixed." "After everything we've given this kid, he's got the nerve to tell you his life isn't worth living!" | Acknowledge the frustration you hear and let the parents talk about it for a while (remember the ways to deal with crisis thinking). Summarize their distress, and review what's been done in the past so you can make a different suggestion for proceeding. If you do have to send them back to a resource they had a bad experience with in the past, offer to make a personal call to see if the agency might be able to respond to this family's needs in a more positive way. |
| 7. Terrified | Especially if there has been a family history of suicide attempts or completions, parents may be extraordinarily fearful and see suicide as inevitable: "Oh my God, we knew this day would come . . ." | Be empathetic to the family's concern. Use that empathy to engage the parents in thinking about what they can do to try to avoid the outcome they fear. Make sure to set up a time to follow up—you want to be sure they get the help they need. |
| 8. Afraid to violate cultural or family norms, or worried about confidentiality concern | Some cultures strongly discourage seeking outside help for what are perceived as personal problems. Other families may be worried about the reaction of extended family members if they pursue professional mental health treatment—"In our family and our culture we take care of our own." There may also be families who worry that mental health treatment may negatively impact their child's future or ability to get into college. | Validate the family's concerns. Try to use a relevant example to make the point that in certain circumstances outside help is necessary. For example, when there's been a car accident, an ambulance is called to transport all the injured to the hospital for assessment and treatment. What's happening to their child is like a car accident in his or her mind—he or she desperately needs professional help to avoid dying. Explain that the referral is not part of the student's transcript and if they don't take care of their child's needs now, he or she might not have a future. |

| Parental Reaction | Explanation | How to Address It |
|---|---|---|
| 9. Need to avoid an underlying family problem or secret | In families that are holding secrets, there may be great unwillingness to let an outsider get too close. Sometimes you get a sense that something is missing as you talk with the parents. They may seem unconcerned, dismissive, eager to get out of your office as quickly as they can. "Thank you so much for your concern—we'll be sure to take care of that right away." | This is often a very tricky situation—your gut tells you something is happening that is different than what is being said or communicated overtly. In the school, it's not your job to figure out the unspoken message. Your best bet with parents like this is to ask their permission to get feedback from the agency that the family showed up for the assessment. Make it clear that all you need is this limited information, but that it's important for school records. |
| 10. Grateful that someone else has validated their concerns about their child | Some families do recognize that something is going on with their child before it is called to their attention by the school, but they may be clueless about how to handle it. They may be relieved to have the school's input and truly appreciate being directed to additional, appropriate resources. | This reaction can provide you with an opportunity to get even more insight into the stresses in a student's life. Explore the reasons for the concerns of the parents, and encourage them to share these with the community referral resource. Explain to the parents that the more information this referral resource has about what's been happening in their child's life, the better able the person or agency will be to provide the kind of help their child needs. |
| 11. Politely let you know that their child is already receiving help | Mental health treatment is often considered a private matter, and many families are reluctant to divulge the fact that their child is already getting treatment. | Thank the parents for their honesty, but remind them of the school's policy regarding at-risk students and the need for a documented assessment of risk by a community mental health resource. |

## GIVEN THIS WIDE RANGE OF REACTIONS, WHAT GUIDELINES ARE THERE FOR A MEETING WITH PARENTS TO DISCUSS THEIR CHILD'S POSSIBLE SUICIDE RISK?

It might help to think of this meeting as having three phases—a beginning, a middle, and an end. Let's consider each of these individually.

### Beginning

1. Although your contact with the parents began when you called to ask them to come in for a meeting, there is something different about meeting face-to-face.

Prepare for the meeting by alerting the office or security staff that you will be meeting with the parents, and ask that you be notified when they arrive or that they be accompanied to your office. Feeling like they are expected can go a long way to decrease the parents' initial anxiety. If you can, post a note on your office door so you won't be interrupted during your meeting.

2. Greet the parents by their last name. ("Hello Mr. and Mrs. Goodman. Thank you for coming in to meet with me.") Introduce yourself if you don't know them. ("I'm Dr. Scott and I'm glad to meet you.")

3. If you can offer a cup of coffee or glass of water, this gesture may also alleviate some anxiety.

4. Clarify the purpose of the meeting and outline its structure. ("I asked you here today to talk about the school's concerns about some things that have been going on with Kate. I'd like to review the reasons why we're worried about Kate, get feedback from you, and then outline plans to help Kate get back on track.")

### *Middle*

1. After you have established rapport and laid out the agenda, move into the middle of the interview where the discussion about the student's suicide risk occurs.

2. Keep the format simple and the discussion on track. Don't get distracted by random remarks or tangential direction. ("I know your older daughter

### What *Not* to Do at a Parent Meeting:

- Call parents by their first names unless they give you permission.
- Be too casual. Their child's behavior is a serious topic and your demeanor should reflect this.
- Self-disclose. The meeting is about them—not the ways in which you may have had similar experiences.
- Ignore resistance. That just makes it worse!
- Rush. Take your time. This is a very important meeting, and your patience speaks to this.
- Answer the phone during your meeting. If you do have to take an important call, explain at the onset of the meeting and apologize for the potential distraction.

had a similar problem, but right now we need to talk about Kate.") The more organized you can be in presenting the facts and data you have accumulated, the easier it will be for parents, especially those who may be in shock, to follow along. ("Let me say again—here's why we're concerned.")

3. Explain that you and the student have already talked about the reasons for concern. In an ideal world, the student will understand why you are worried about him or her and provide additional insight into his or her current emotional state. If the student disagrees with the school's observations, explain to the parents and student that this is another reason to have a more comprehensive evaluation by an objective, off-campus mental health professional.

4. Allow the parents time to react to the information you have presented within the meeting. Appreciate that these disclosures may have taken them by surprise, but convey the urgency of getting an evaluation as soon as possible because of your concern about suicide. Make sure to have an action plan before they leave the meeting.

5. If you feel the student is at *imminent* risk for suicide, make this very clear to the parents. Be sure they understand that their child requires an assessment this very day, and give them the name of an emergency facility where this can be accomplished. Reinforce that you are concerned for their child's *safety* and that it is *urgent* that a comprehensive evaluation be completed right away! Offer to alert the emergency resource that the student is on the way and to provide the reasons for the school's concerns. Recognize that in most states students will not receive emergency treatment without parental permission, so it is essential that they accompany their child to the emergency resource.

6. Be clear with parents if school policy requires a written release from the professional completing the evaluation before the student will be allowed to return to school.

7. Provide the parents with a list of recommended community resources for this assessment. Encourage them to sign a written release to give the evaluator permission to share limited information about the student with the school.

***End***

1. Summarize the key points of the meeting. ("So it sounds like we're all on the same page. You're clear that here at the school we're concerned about Kate because her performance has really declined but, even more importantly, because she admits that she has been so distressed that she has been having thoughts about taking her life. I've given you the name of a facility that can conduct a more complete risk assessment this afternoon,

and as soon as you leave I'll call to let them know you're on your way with Kate. Have I got it right so far?") Provide the parents and the student with an opportunity to add or correct information or to ask questions.

2. Explain that school protocol requires parents to sign a form indicating they have understood the reasons for the school's concerns and confirming that they will be taking the student for a more comprehensive evaluation. This form should include a summary of your district's policy regarding students who are identified as at risk for self-harm or suicide, as well as contact information at the school in case the referral resource or parents have additional questions. A twenty-four-hour hotline number should also be provided on the form. The form should be signed by both the school counselor completing the school assessment and the parents. A sample form is included on the CD-ROM for review. Tell the parents you would like to follow up with them to see how things are going and to check in on how they and their child are doing.

**7-2**

## SHOULD THE STUDENT ALWAYS BE IN THE MEETING?

Generally, it is helpful to have the student sit in on at least part, if not all, of the meeting. It communicates that the school is joining with the student's parents to problem-solve a more effective solution for the student's current distress. Having the student remain in the room when the parents are there eliminates questions about what was said by whom; the communication is open and clear. This can be especially helpful with older students who may have difficulty trusting the intentions of either the school or their parents to help them better manage their level of distress.

With younger elementary and middle school students, there may be issues parents want to discuss more confidentially. Worries about sexual identity, the impact of learning disorders on classroom performance, issues related to early puberty, the effect of impending family changes like divorce or separation—these are examples of the topics parents may want to talk about privately with the counselor. While the student may be excused from this section of the meeting, it is generally a good call to invite the student back when referral recommendations and plans for follow-up are summarized. (Of course, the student must stay in a safe and supervised location until he or she is invited back into the room.) It's important that the plans are clear to everyone and that the student has the opportunity to ask questions about the process from his or her perspective.

## HOW DO I ADDRESS ACCESS TO MEANS, SUCH AS PILLS OR A GUN, WITH THE PARENTS?

Obviously, knowing that a student has access to the means to harm himself or herself sets up an immediate red flag for an emergency mental health referral. In situations like this, call the referral resource from your office to set up the appointment so there is little doubt that the family will follow through. It's also important to instruct the family to remove the dangerous means. Especially if the youth has access to firearms, these *must* be removed from the premises. If one of the parents is required to carry a firearm as part of his or her job, suggest that it be locked in the trunk of the car until the suicide crisis has passed. Simply dismantling guns or hiding ammunition may not be enough.

*"The guns in our house were locked in a cabinet in the den. We hid the key. There was no way Beau knew where it was, so he took the hinges off the cabinet and stole a revolver. That's what he used to kill himself."*

—MOTHER OF SEVENTEEN-YEAR-OLD BOY WHO DIED BY SUICIDE

It's also important to clear the house of potentially harmful medication. This includes both prescriptions and over-the-counter drugs that can be dangerous if taken in large quantities. One of the drugs essential to remove is Tylenol, which is often the overdose drug of choice for young teens. It contains acetaminophen, which can cause permanent liver damage when taken even in small amounts. The person or agency to whom you are referring the family for additional at-risk assessment should give the family these same instructions. This information is so important it cannot be conveyed too often!

*"Chloe was referred by her Spanish teacher because she seemed 'out of it' in class. When she arrived at my office she seemed distracted and admitted she was upset that her ex-boyfriend had been spreading nasty rumors about her around school. When I questioned her about how distracted she seemed to be, she admitted she had taken a few pills to calm herself down. While her answers were initially vague and confusing, she finally admitted she had taken about fifteen extra-strength Tylenol. 'I feel fine' she kept insisting when I told her she had taken a potentially lethal dose and needed to go to the hospital immediately.*

*Following our school policy, I immediately called her parents and 9-1-1. When her parents brought the empty bottle to the hospital, they determined Chloe had taken twenty-four pills, a decidedly fatal dose."*

—HIGH SCHOOL STUDENT ASSISTANCE COUNSELOR

## WHAT INFORMATION CAN HELP EXPLAIN THE BASICS OF MENTAL HEALTH TREATMENT TO PARENTS?

**7-3**

Many parents have very little experience accessing or using mental health services. If you are encouraging parents to have their child evaluated for mental health treatment, they may find even thinking about making the first appointment bewildering and overwhelming. You will find answers to questions frequently asked by parents who are seeking mental health treatment for their children on the CD-ROM. You may wish to incorporate this information into your parent meeting and/or provide the information as a handout. It would also be extremely helpful to compile information about your local mental health resources into a handout for parents.

Now let's look at information that can help you answer questions that parents might ask about suicide risk evaluation and treatment.

## WHAT KINDS OF EVALUATION AND TREATMENT ARE SUGGESTED FOR A CHILD WHO IS SUICIDAL?

An evaluation for suicide risk is very similar to the type of mental health evaluation provided when a child is referred under other circumstances. If there is a question about suicide, however, this assessment will also include specific and detailed questions related to both risk for and warning signs of suicide. Some mental health practitioners will ask the child to complete a paper-and-pencil questionnaire to help them determine the *level of risk*. If the child is determined to be at low or moderate risk, treatment will be managed on an outpatient basis, and a treatment strategy will be developed that includes a safety plan—specific ways in which the child can respond if he or she continues to have thoughts and feelings about suicide, as well as emergency contact information. In the case of imminent risk, the assessment will also include a determination of whether the child may need hospitalization until the suicide crisis has diminished. When the benefits of treatment with medication outweigh the risks, psychotropic or antidepressant medication might also be recommended.

## WHAT IS MEANT BY A "BLACK BOX" WARNING RELATED TO THE USE OF PSYCHOTROPIC MEDICATIONS FOR CHILDREN?

In 2004, the U.S. Food and Drug Administration (FDA) mandated that all antidepressant medication prescribed to children and adolescents indicate that use of this medication could result in an increase in suicidal ideation or suicide attempts. This warning was based on studies that showed 2 to 3 percent of pediatric patients experienced an increase in suicidal thoughts during the first four weeks of use. Although there was not a single completed suicide in the studies, the "black box" warning does call attention to the importance of making sure that children or adolescents who are taking antidepressant medication are closely monitored by the prescribing physician early in the course of treatment or when medication is adjusted or changed. Since 2004, there has been a stream of additional research on the effects of antidepressant medication on children and teens. It's important to encourage parents to ask the prescribing physician about the implications of the most current research on the effects of these drugs, so they can make informed decisions about their child's medical treatment. Remind them that they would do the same thing if their child were prescribed a drug for a physical condition; this is no different.

## IF THIS TYPE OF MEDICATION CAN BE SO DANGEROUS, WHY IS IT PRESCRIBED?

While medication isn't usually necessary for milder forms of depression, it can be a very important and effective component in treatment of children and teens who are severely depressed. Untreated clinical depression can be extremely incapacitating for kids, creating symptoms that interfere with their ability to perform in school and athletics, maintain friendships, interact at home . . . the list goes on. Explain to parents that neither they nor you are in a position to make the medical diagnosis of depression, which is why it's so important to consult with a community mental health professional. If the mental health professional recommends the use of antidepressant medication, he or she will either prescribe it (if the professional has prescribing privileges) or refer the family to a physician (such as a psychiatrist or pediatrician) for treatment. No matter who prescribes the medication, instruct parents to ask for the following:

- information that helps them understand depression as an illness
- clarification of the risks and signs of suicidality
- information that addresses the benefits and risks of medication
- facts about the medication's side effects, as well as what to do about them

In addition, tell parents to make sure to discuss how the doctor will monitor both the introduction of the medication and the evaluation of its effectiveness. Parents need to ask the physician to clarify their responsibility for monitoring the medication and to estimate the length of time the child may need to take the medication. Even though it may seem premature, finding out the process for discontinuation of the medication is also useful. And, simple as it may seem, parents should find out the best time of the day for taking the medication. Even when they have sought professional help for their child, parents need to continue to monitor the effects of the medication, be alert for side effects, and, if they're concerned about the progress of treatment, consider getting a second opinion. The bottom line is to encourage parents not to be just consumers, but *educated* consumers.

Despite these caveats, however, it's important to remind parents that when the benefits of medication outweigh the risks, antidepressants—when carefully monitored by patient, family, and physician—have proven to be very effective in the treatment of depression.

## SO IF MEDICATION IS EFFECTIVE, DO KIDS NEED ANYTHING ELSE?

Yes! Medication is only one piece of the treatment equation. Several studies have shown that a combination of medication and talk therapy (counseling) is really the most successful form of treatment. As of this date, research studies have demonstrated that the most effective treatment for depressed teens is cognitive behavioral therapy, or CBT. Very simply, CBT first helps teens identify the thoughts and behaviors that are causing them to feel depressed. They then learn how to correct those depressed thinking patterns, activate healthier and more functional behavior, and practice positive problem-solving skills.

## LET'S REVIEW

Involving parents or guardians in the process of getting help for a potentially suicidal student is an essential part of the progression from school to community assessment resources. Knowing how to engage parents, however, can sometimes be challenging. This chapter reviewed reasons behind what may seem like parental reluctance or resistance to accepting the school's observations that their child may be at risk for suicide. It also offered strategies for dealing with these potential roadblocks. Although the topics covered in this chapter are by no means exhaustive, they should provide you with a framework for organizing your responses to the parents you will see in your office.

Since a key piece of resistance may be lack of information about the mental health system, this chapter also addressed common questions asked by parents about mental health resources.

The next chapter will outline considerations in the referral process itself and offer techniques for setting the stage for productive referrals to community mental health resources.

## IN YOUR
# Experience . . .

- Think about challenging parents you've dealt with. How did you respond to them? Did this chapter give you ideas of how you might have handled the situations differently?

- What are the things you already do to prepare to call or meet with parents? What makes these things work?

- How prepared do you feel to address questions about mental health treatment and medication? What more do you need to know to feel more comfortable discussing these issues with parents?

## RESOURCES

Association for Behavioral and Cognitive Therapies and the Society of Clinical Child and Adolescent Psychology. "Evidence-based Mental Healthy Treatment for Children and Adolescents." See www.effectivechildtherapy.com.

National Association of Cognitive-Behavioral Therapist. "What Is Cognitive Behavioral Therapy?" See www.nacbt.org/whatiscbt.htm.

National Institute of Mental Health. "How to Find Help." See www.nimh.nih.gov /health/topics/getting-help-locate-services/index.shtml.

NYU Child Study Center. See www.aboutourkids.org.

## HANDOUTS

7-1: Common Reactions from Parents Who Have Been Informed That Their Child Is Suicidal

7-2: Referral Information for Parents: Student Risk Assessment

7-3: Questions Frequently Asked by Parents about Mental Health Treatment

# Chapter 8

# Putting It Together: Making Effective Referrals

*"I have learned from experience that making good referrals is not as easy as it looks—there's a lot of work that needs to be done up front. I've got to know my resources and make sure they've got the time to see a student as soon as possible. The second thing I've learned is that even if I know at the beginning of a student contact that this is a kid who is going to need an emergency assessment for suicide risk immediately, it's always better if all parties—the student and the parents—buy into the idea. Being able to provide information about where I want to send them can be a big piece of that buy-in. It takes a little more work, but in the long run, it's so much more effective than making a blind referral and sending the student to an unknown name on a referral list."*

*—SCHOOL PSYCHOLOGIST*

Getting students to needed mental health resources generally involves more than just meeting with the student and the parents to explain the necessity for more assessment and evaluation than the school can provide. Making effective referrals for community services can be a time-consuming process. With all of the other responsibilities that crowd the daily schedules of school resource staff, the thought of making exploratory contact with community referral resources may seem like a great idea in theory but impossible in practice. And yet, as we listen to the voice of the school psychologist who opens this chapter, we can all agree that personally knowing where you're sending a student, especially one who is suicidal, might go a long way in quickly facilitating the collaboration that creates a stronger safety net for an at-risk youth.

School personnel often have to make referrals to community services for a wide variety of problems that commonly surface among their students. In fact, any community consists of a *network* of services and agencies that constantly refer clients to each other. Although making referrals is a common activity, it is done with varying degrees of success. It is not always easy to make a referral that is equally acceptable to the person being referred and the person or agency receiving the referral. Accomplishing this involves not only obtaining the right services for the student but also maintaining open communication and smooth working relationships with other agencies.

Referring an adolescent for counseling or other mental health services, in fact, turns out to be one of the more difficult transitions to accomplish. Research has shown that few of these referrals are followed up on or, if the adolescent does complete an initial appointment, he or she often fails to return for subsequent appointments.

While a good referral is always important, it takes on an added degree of urgency when it involves a suicidal student. This chapter will identify reasons for ineffective referrals and will outline strategies for addressing them and ensuring that the referral has a better chance of follow-through. It will also summarize content from previous chapters to create a template that reflects all of the necessary ingredients in an optimal referral.

By the end of this chapter, you will be able to

- outline what makes some referrals more successful than others

- understand the importance of engaging students and parents in the referral process

- list strategies for making more successful referrals

- use a checklist of questions to determine the applicability of referral resources to the school's needs

## WHAT ARE THE REASONS FOR MISSTEPS IN THE REFERRAL PROCESS?

There are *many* reasons numerous referrals of youth for mental health treatment are unsuccessful. The challenges fall on all sides of the process—the way in which the referral is made, the way the parents and/or students perceive the referral, and the effectiveness of the referral resource in meeting the child's and the family's needs.

An effective referral is defined as one that seems acceptable or appropriate to the person making the referral, the person or agency receiving the referral, and at least to some degree, the student and parents who are being referred. Despite the challenges, there are ways of making referrals that increase the likelihood of a successful transition from the school counselor to a community resource.

These strategies can be roughly divided into three categories:

1. Involving the student in the referral

2. Involving the parents in the referral

3. Considerations involved in the actual referral process

## HOW DO I INVOLVE A STUDENT IN THE PROCESS?

Setting the stage for involving the student in the referral process begins during the "Tell Me More" assessment and includes the following two steps:

### 1. Clarifying the Problem

This may sound obvious, but it is not uncommon for referrals to be made before the problem has been clarified. This results in inappropriate referrals that distress the student and his or her family, the community referral resource, and you. By taking the time to listen and clarify the concerns, you accomplish at least four things:

- First, you obtain the information you need to support your decision to refer and to help you make the best referral you can.

- Second, you show the student that you have listened to his or her concerns and are incorporating them into your recommendation.

- Third, you demonstrate a willingness to understand the student's perspective, thus establishing some rapport that may make it easier for the student to accept your suggestions or directions. Even if you know that the student needs additional help before he or she walks into your office, take the time to listen to the student's side of the story. While setting the stage for the referral takes place throughout your intervention with the student, making the actual referral works best at the end of a process, not the beginning. This timing reinforces that you've taken into consideration everything the student has said to make the most appropriate referral.

- Fourth, you can reinforce that you are sending the student *to* a valuable resource and not just *away from* you. It's important to keep this fact in the front of your mind when making a student referral. Students often assume that talking with you is the *last* step in the process, not the *first*. Being informed that they're going to have to tell their story to someone else can be discouraging, so it's helpful to remind them throughout your meeting that, although the school's resources are limited, you know a lot of good places in the community where they will be able to get the help they need. You'll hear this point reiterated throughout this chapter because it is so essential to making a referral that includes follow-through.

*"Even though I told my counselor I was pretty upset about my grandpa's death, she didn't give me a chance to tell her I was going to this grief program at my church and I thought it was really helpful. She just called my mom and told her I needed to see some kind of grief counselor. I already am getting grief counseling!"*

—TEN-YEAR-OLD BOY

*"So when Mr. K asked me to talk about my problems, it was hard to tell him at first. I mean, I'm the kind of kid who keeps things to myself. So it took me a while to get up the courage to explain what was happening, but I felt so good after I did! Then when my parents got there, Mr. K. told them I had to talk to someone else. I didn't understand why Mr. K couldn't be the person to help me. Then Mr. K explained that school isn't always the best place for that sort of thing since it can be hard to have the time you need to really be able to discuss what's bothering you 'cause of the schedules and other kids interrupting and stuff like that. I guess that makes sense. But Mr. K told me he'd check back with me to see how I like this other counselor and that made me feel better."*

—KEVIN, THIRTEEN-YEAR-OLD BOY

Obviously, it's important for the student to know early on that the school's resources for helping are limited, but the timing of that revelation is sensitive. If you tell the student as soon as he or she walks in the door, it may seem like there's no point talking to you. If you tell the student too late, he or she may feel cheated and tricked. Recall in the last chapter when we discussed how families tend to keep personal problems to themselves and may be reluctant to let outsiders in on their struggles. Kids can feel the same way. The way in which you handle your initial request for them to open up to you should also reflect your desire to help them find the best available help for their problems. If your school has a health clinic that provides mental health services, that assistance may be within the school, but more often than not, it will require the use of community resources.

## 2. Addressing Any Reluctance

Some students may find a referral to an off-campus counselor a relief. Others, however, may be quite hesitant. The first step is to find out how the student feels about the referral. A simple way to address this is to ask, "How does this sound to you?" or "How do you feel about my suggesting this?" or "How do you feel about talking to a psychologist or a social worker?" Pay attention to nonverbal cues such as tone of voice and body language, as well as to what the student says.

There's a range of understandable feelings that may interfere with the student's acceptance of the referral. These feelings include the following:

- Rejection: "Why can't you help me?"

- Hopelessness: "If you can't help me, nobody can!" "Going for counseling means I'm sicker than I thought."

- Frustration: "I've been to a counselor before and all she did was take my parents' money." "All shrinks do is prescribe drugs."

- Anger: "I thought you were supposed to help me." "I'm tired of telling my story." "You're just trying to get rid of me."

- Fear: "My parents will kill me if they find out I told someone all of this." "They told me if I cause one more problem, I'm out on my ear." "You're crazier than I am if you think my dad would pay for a shrink."

- Embarrassment: "If my friends ever found out I was seeing a shrink, I'd never hear the end of it."

It's very important to address any concerns you pick up on that reflect reluctance to follow up on your referral. Ignoring the student's feelings doesn't make them go away. And you can't simply acknowledge them ("I can appreciate you don't want to tell your story again"); you need to *address* and *respond* to them specifically. Addressing them provides the opportunity to

- clear up misconceptions and speak to the student's fears about being abandoned by you

- address the student's concerns about mental health treatment

- explore worries about parental and peer reactions

In addition to responding to the student's concerns, you may indicate, as the counselor did in the example of Kevin, that you intend to check back with the student to find out how the referral is going.

*"I cried in the doctor's office and he is so used to patients crying that it didn't even affect him. I tried to hold back the tears, but I'm so exhausted, and while I was talking they were just running out of my eyes. He didn't give me tissues or ask if I was okay, and once he gave me the new medication, he just opened the door and made me walk out in front of everyone with all my tears. I was even more upset that maybe there would be someone I knew in the waiting room who might see me. So when my school counselor asked how the meeting went, I told him and I think he called the doctor, because he was much nicer to me the next time I went to see him."*

—FOURTEEN-YEAR-OLD GIRL

## DO STUDENTS WORRY THAT THEIR PEERS MIGHT FIND OUT THEY'RE SEEING A MENTAL HEALTH COUNSELOR?

Yes. For many teens, having peers know that they see a counselor may be the ultimate embarrassment, so reassuring teens about privacy and confidentiality concerns is a critical step in getting them to consider mental health treatment. Even if they don't verbalize their worries about these issues, many kids, especially boys, believe that seeking mental health counseling will make them look weak or crazy in the eyes of their peers. Explain that counselors understand these feelings and try hard to schedule appointments to ensure as much privacy as possible. It's also important to encourage the student to share these concerns with the counselor. Emphasize that all records are kept confidential and that, unless a counselor is worried that the student's safety or the safety of others is in jeopardy, everything that happens in the counseling session remains between the student and the counselor.

Sometimes, however, despite your best efforts, the student remains unconvinced about the need for a referral. At this point, it may be best to acknowledge your disagreement, indicate that you have to follow school policy, and invite the student to share his or her concerns with the mental health counselor. If the student at least feels he or she has been listened to, the transition to a community provider may be better accepted. Students can hold the belief that you had no choice but to follow school policies and protocols if that perception remains helpful to them.

As you know, teens often listen best to their peers, so one other thing that might be helpful is to share the experience another teen had with a mental health counselor. Nadia, the teen in the following example, had made several suicide attempts and was hospitalized for three months in a psychiatric hospital. This was how she responded on her blog when asked about her experiences with a counselor:

> "They don't judge (appear to judge) and they don't hold anything against you no matter how emotional or blunt you are. The worst parts (for me) are: (1) the waiting room and (2) when you leave and you feel the same as when you walked in. I know it's stupid but I kind of expected that I would start to feel better instantly, but it doesn't work that way. It takes time and effort. Unfortunately. I really don't want to make it sound like a bad thing—I'm just trying to be honest. It couldn't be easier though, and there really is nothing to worry about.

> "Forget about what you've seen in movies; You go in, you sit down, she/he maps out a general summary of your life and your daily routine. You talk about how you are feeling and how you want to feel, and by that time it's the end of your first session.

> "After that, it's all plans and feelings and suggestions. You don't have to do anything that you don't want to and you don't have to be open right away—they understand that it takes time. Don't settle for someone you don't feel comfortable with and don't hesitate to tell them if you don't like what they are saying or asking."

Sharing honest, yet hopeful, guidance from other young people with experience in mental health counseling can be helpful in getting a teen to go to at least the first counseling appointment. (A great online resource for this type of peer support and reassurance is reachout.com.) After that, it's up to the counselor to whom you make the referral to engage the teen in the ongoing counseling process. When the referral is for an emergency screening, of course, this engagement is of less concern than the assessment for imminent suicide risk. But when you're referring a low- or moderate-risk student for counseling, establishing rapport is an essential step in convincing the student that he or she has something to gain from the counseling process. You can easily check up on this when you see the student for the first follow-up. Ask simple questions like these: "What did you think of the counselor?" "Did you feel like she connected with you?" or "How do you feel about going back?" These questions are a good barometer for measuring whether the counselor has begun to engage the student in the intervention.

## ARE THE STEPS FOR INVOLVING PARENTS IN THE REFERRAL THE SAME AS THEY ARE FOR STUDENTS?

While the principles are obviously similar—clarify the problem and address any reluctance—your school may have specific procedures for contacting parents. The strategies we suggest were covered in detail in chapter 7.

To briefly review, an appropriate first step is a phone call to let parents know that you are concerned about their child and to ask them to come in for a conversation. As emphasized before, make sure you have as much objective evidence as possible to support your concerns. It is best to briefly state what you have *seen* that causes you concern (rather than imply what the causes for the behavior might be); then ask the parents if this fits with anything they have seen or know that has been going on with the student. This technique invites the parents to join with you in a discussion about their child, rather than receiving a "report card" from you.

After you have spelled out the reasons for your concern, you will want to make a referral to the type of community intervention that best meets the student's needs. As most school officials know, many parents will quickly accept a referral suggestion. With parents who may be resistant, you may need to restate your concerns several times before they sink in. With some parents, you may need to appeal to their parenting: "I know you want to do what's best for your child." Unfortunately, with others you may have to resort to pointing out possible consequences of not taking action at this time.

> *Counselor:* I realize you don't see your son's behavior as being as serious as we do, but unfortunately, we've known families that have felt the way you do and have had children who have gone on to make suicide attempts.

> *or*

> *Counselor:* I will respectfully disagree with your feelings that we are making something out of nothing and leave it to a mental health professional to make that decision for both of us.

As with the student, sometimes even your best efforts may leave the parents unconvinced of the need for a referral. This presents a substantial dilemma when you feel that the risk of a suicide attempt is high or when there has been an actual attempt.

When faced with the situation of parents who refuse to comply with the school's request for an evaluation, school officials must consider involving a child protection agency. States have different laws regarding the involvement of a child protection agency, and there is even greater variance in their application to suicidal risk, as opposed to physical abuse. In these circumstances, you will want to involve your school administration, possibly in consultation with your school board attorney, to recommend a course of action.

## EVEN WHEN A STUDENT AND FAMILY AGREE TO A REFERRAL, HOW DO I KNOW THE BEST PLACE TO SEND THEM?

As the example at the beginning of this chapter demonstrated, knowing something about the place or the person to whom you are making a referral is one of the best strategies for successfully fulfilling your role in the referral process.

**8-1**

Here are some additional suggestions to make the transition to community resources work more smoothly. You can also find this list on the CD-ROM. As you'll see, the suggestions are aimed not only at making better referrals for students and parents but also at maintaining good working relationships with these community services.

a. Know your local mental health resources. Some communities may have only one agency that provides mental health services, but many communities have a variety of agencies that meet these needs (local community mental health center, family services agency, crisis services, and so on). Some agencies may even have special services for adolescents. An awareness of community resources will help you in making a referral that best meets the student's needs. A personal contact or liaison with a staff member in these agencies can also facilitate the referral process.

b. Create memorandums of understanding with a range of agencies that can serve your students' needs. The memorandums of understanding should contain clear statements about confidentiality between the agencies, the school, the students, and the families. Having these relationships and expectations arranged in advance makes the transition smoother for the families.

c. In cases when you refer a student to be evaluated for suicide risk, you need to make sure that the person or agency to whom you refer has the capability to hospitalize the student if it seems necessary. Referring to an agency or person without that capacity (clergy, mental health clinic without psychiatric hospital affiliation) just adds another step to the process at a point when timely action is indicated. There is nothing quite so frustrating to a family you have convinced to get crisis assessment than to have to shuttle from one place to another in search of the most appropriate resource. So when you're checking out referral resources, make sure to inquire about their capacity to respond to situations of imminent suicide risk.

> ### Referral Resource Guidelines
>
> - Know local resources
> - Verify resource capacity
> - Be selective
> - Match the family to the resource
> - Call the referral resource yourself when there is imminent suicide risk
> - Give the family adequate contact information for the referral resource
> - Don't promise specific services
> - Don't make "off the record" comments about mental health resources
> - Follow up

Also make sure to find out about waiting lists for services and how a referral for suicidal risk is managed under those conditions. Ask about the wait for services if the suicide risk level is determined to be low or moderate. Especially with adolescents, having to wait for needed services can foster additional resistance to a process about which they are already skeptical.

*"So my school counselor convinces me, somewhat against my will I might add, that I need to talk to someone to work through some things that are bothering me. My parents and I go to this clinic place where I start to tell my story again, and then they tell me I have to wait like two months to talk to a real counselor. Forget about it!"*

—ROCCO, FIFTEEN YEARS OLD

    **d.** Even if a variety of community resources could provide the service the student needs, it is best to select just one or two for your referral. A large number of choices can be confusing at a time when the family's decision-making ability may already be taxed. Make it clear, however, that you are simply providing the family with suggestions for referrals, not requiring that the family use any particular community resource. You may explain that the school has had more experience working with some mental health care providers than with others, but that as long as the person or place the parents will be taking their child has the expertise to provide a risk assessment for suicide, any choice they make will be fine. If they decide to use a referral resource of their own choosing, remind them to inquire about the ability to perform a specific risk assessment for suicide since not every mental health resource will have that capacity.

e. Try to match the family with the resource available. Anticipate difficulties if the community agency to which you normally make this type of referral is geographically distant, the family lacks transportation, or the agency doesn't meet the insurance requirements of the family. Check for other more local resources that may provide that service. It will require your spending extra time now, but it could save you time later if the family finds it simply impossible to get to the location. If possible, use a referral that fits the family's background and resources (religious affiliation, cultural background, financial resources). For example, don't send a low-income family to a private practitioner who may be very skilled but whom the family can't afford.

*"I'm sure the school counselor was trying to be really helpful, but she got us an appointment at a place that didn't take our insurance. We don't have out-of-network benefits, so we had to pay what was a fortune to us for an evaluation because we were so worried our son might kill himself. They were really good and my son liked the counselor a lot, but we can't afford to go back there."*

*—PARENT OF SEVENTEEN-YEAR-OLD*

f. Doing your homework about your referral resource can be really important. Especially in a school, it is important to get informal feedback from students about the people and places to which you send them. Listen to what one student told her school social worker when asked about a psychologist in the community to whom she had been referred:

> "I told her that I felt like my world was falling apart, I told her that I didn't know how much longer I could hang on, I told her that I feel like I'm carrying the weight of the world and it's crushing me, and then she asked me if I'd been doing my breathing exercises. Enough said."

g. If you feel that the situation is an emergency, set up the referral yourself before the family leaves your office. Call the community referral resource and let the staff know you are sending the family immediately for an evaluation. Again, be clear about your reasons for the referral. As stated earlier, it is important that the parents accompany the student to the evaluation, as services are often not provided to adolescents without parental permission.

**h.** If you feel comfortable letting the family set up the appointment, make sure to give the complete information about the referral. This includes the name of a person at the agency to contact, phone number, address, directions from school or home, information about cost, and so on.

**i.** Do not commit your community referral resource to a specific course of action by implying or promising to the student or parents that the agency will definitely work with the teen, hospitalize or not hospitalize, and the like. Your previous arrangements with the referral agency will only ensure that staff will see the student. After that, the agency must be free to decide the most appropriate course of action.

**j.** It is best not to make evaluative comments about other agencies or individuals in your community. Any questions about the competence, responsiveness, and so on, of specific agencies or individuals are best deflected with the statement that you are only familiar with the ability of those agencies to respond to the school's request for services. That being said, if a student or parent returns with a complaint or concern about your referral resource, obtain specific details, and follow up immediately with that agency to clarify any misunderstandings about services or procedures.

**k.** Indicate to the parents and student your intention to follow up with them and the referral resource. Ask the parents to sign a release of information at the referral agency to allow you to receive limited information about the outcome of the evaluation. Explain that it is imperative that the school coordinate its response to their child with the mental health professional who is making the assessment in order to continue to provide a supportive environment for their child. Without the family's specific written consent, this will be impossible. Let the family know that you only need information that relates to the treatment plan, not details about the specific problem or the family.

> ### Questions to Ask Referral Services When Creating a Resource Referral List
>
> - Do you have staff with child/adolescent experience or training?
> - Does your staff reflect the ethnic diversity of the community?
> - How long does it take to get an intake appointment?
> - What are your procedures for youth who may need hospitalization?
> - Do you have staff who can prescribe medication if it's needed?
> - What insurance plans to you accept? Do you accept Medicaid? Do you adjust your fees for clients without insurance coverage?
> - Do you have protocols or memorandums of understanding for collaborating with the school to provide coordinated support for the student?

## WHAT DO SCHOOL FACULTY AND STAFF NEED TO KNOW ABOUT POTENTIALLY SUICIDAL STUDENTS?

It may sound evasive to talk about giving information on a need-to-know basis, but like many of the issues involved in suicide intervention and prevention, there isn't a simple, clear-cut answer. The most honest answer to what other faculty in a school need to know about a potentially at-risk student is: it depends. It depends on the level of risk.

- Many students, in every school in the country, exhibit *low levels of suicide risk*. Most of these students will escape your notice. Those who do come to the attention of the school can be referred to community resources for additional assessment and treatment evaluation. Generally, there will not be a need to disseminate information about these students to faculty or other school staff.

- Students at *moderate risk* may come to the attention of school faculty and staff. Along with a referral to local mental health resources for further assessment, ask the parents/guardians to sign a release so the community referral resource can communicate back to the school what kinds of support may be most helpful. For example, a classroom teacher may need to know whether school assignments, test schedules, and so on should be adjusted and whether the student can complete regular assignments. The school nurse should know about medications and when they are to be taken. Such information should be shared in private, never in a faculty lounge discussion. Faculty and staff members who do not interact directly with the student should not be offered information without a genuine need to know. If there is an emergent need or concern, the faculty member should be instructed to contact the school-based resource staff member assigned to monitor the student's progress.

- Students at *high risk* will most likely be sent to a facility for assessment of imminent risk and possible hospitalization. From the perspective of most schools, the most appropriate—and necessary—treatment is to hospitalize the student until his or her safety can be assured. However, from the mental health perspective, the treatment standard that is applied is called "the least restrictive." This means that even though the student may be at a high risk for suicide, the evaluators have determined that he or she can be managed in an outpatient setting and not need hospitalization. When this happens, it can be confusing and frustrating for school staff. In the case of high-risk students, faculty who interact with the student *must* be alerted to watch for any escalation of suicide warning signs and informed of the process of what to do and who to alert if a concern does arise. If a student is hospitalized, a reintegration plan should be implemented to improve the success of transition back into school. More information about how to create this reintegration plan is provided in chapter 9.

*"Sending students to be evaluated at our local emergency room was very frustrating. Even though students would tell us at school that they had been thinking about suicide and had a clear plan, we would send them for an evaluation in the afternoon and they'd be back in school the next day. A week later we'd be sending them out again and the same thing would happen. It made us crazy! So our director of counseling had a meeting with the administrators at the hospital to try to figure out how to make the system work better. What we realized was that we weren't sending enough information to the hospital about the reasons for our concerns. When the students would get to the hospital, they'd give half the story and it wouldn't sound nearly as serious as it had at school. Knowing that helped us a lot. So we developed a form that included more comprehensive referral information. There were still kids we thought should be hospitalized that weren't, but we felt that now at least our referrals were taken seriously. When students were placed in outpatient*

*treatment rather than inpatient, we'd try to talk with the outpatient therapist to see how we could become involved in the treatment plan. It took a while to work it all out, but the system sure works better now!"*

—SCHOOL PSYCHOLOGIST

## WHAT DO SCHOOLS NEED FROM THEIR MENTAL HEALTH RESOURCES TO MAKE THE REFERRAL PROCESS WORK MORE SMOOTHLY?

It is imperative for schools to have some information that allows them to provide appropriate supports for the student and to avoid conflicts with the mental health treatment plan. Unfortunately, some mental health agencies do not provide vital information to the schools about the ways in which they can support the student, because the community agency considers sharing of this information to be a breach of their client's confidentiality. This issue should be resolved when establishing a working relationship between the school and the local mental health care provider (perhaps spelled out in the memorandum of understanding) and prior to an actual referral.

Some schools have policies that they will not accept a student back into the school after a suicide attempt if such information and joint planning is not in place. Again, having clear prior arrangements and solid working relationships with community agencies will make this collaborative process a lot easier.

## LET'S REVIEW

One of the more challenging parts of the assessment process can be making an effective referral. Knowing where to send a potentially at-risk student is only one part of the successful referral equation. Convincing the student and his or her parents to follow through on your recommendations is just as essential and is more easily accomplished when you make them partners in the process. Exploring and addressing both student and parental resistance to referral may take a little time. But in the end, this may be what makes the difference in their compliance with your referral suggestion.

Make sure your referral resource is relevant, culturally competent, and appropriate to the particular student's needs. Stay on top of your community resources and keep your list of referral resources current. Particularly with a student who may be suicidal, your referral may open the door to lifesaving resources, so give it the care it deserves!

## IN YOUR
# Experience . . .

- How recently have you updated your list of referrals?
- Do your community referrals routinely ask parents to sign releases to facilitate your collaboration with them?
- If you experience difficulty in having at-risk kids hospitalized, have you asked your administrators to help the school address this?

## HANDOUTS

8-1: Considerations in the Mental Health Referral Process

# Chapter 9

# Special Challenges in Intervention

*"After twenty years as a school social worker in a large, suburban district, I've had a lot of experience with what we call the more 'typical' kids who present with suicide risk. These kids are challenging enough to deal with. But when students with complicating factors—like being bullied, for example—present to us, I know I'm always a little more anxious that I may be missing something or that I'm not up on the current research. And if my anxiety goes up, I know that doesn't help the student in the least!"*

*—SCHOOL SOCIAL WORKER*

There's no way that even the most competent and conscientious school resource staff member would have the time to keep up with the emerging body of research on suicide risk for youth. And believe it or not, that's actually the good news. Twenty-five years ago, for example, research on youth suicide was in its infancy and very little information was available to guide schools in making informed decisions about the at-risk youth in their student population. We have certainly learned enough since then to understand the ways in which schools can become competent and compassionate communities that are actively concerned about the welfare of all their members, especially potentially at-risk youth. And while an evidence-based body of knowledge about suicidality remains consistent for all youth, some particular groups of students can benefit from a specialized review of current research and theory. Students in these groups tend to feel "different" from their peers and often are subject to harassment and discrimination, which can increase their risk not only for suicide but also for other self-destructive behaviors. These groups include

- students returning to school after being hospitalized for a suicide attempt

- gifted and talented students

- students who are bullied

- sexual minority students

- special education students

This chapter includes five sections, each addressing unique issues encountered by students in each of these populations. Each section begins with the personal story of a student and then adds specific information about unique risk or protective factors and current research or recommended program initiatives for that particular group of students.

It's important to remember, however, that whatever the unique characteristics or circumstances presented by a particular student, the rules for student engagement, parental contact, and subsequent referral are always the same. So, too, is the suggestion outlined in chapter 2 that you get in touch with your personal values, attitudes, and beliefs about the student and his or her particular situation. The students discussed in this chapter are usually in even greater need of support, acceptance, and encouragement than the general school population. If a counselor conveys disapproval or disdain, it could be devastating for students who already feel shaky about who they are and how they are perceived.

That being said, it is also essential to keep in mind that most of the students in these subgroups navigate adolescence safely and even smoothly. Every student we meet, regardless of special characteristics, needs to be perceived as a unique individual who may or may not be at risk.

By the end of this chapter, you will be able to

- identify the unique risk factors in special populations of students

- develop strategies to support these students

- consider the ways in which the environment in your school supports or discourages these students

# STUDENTS RETURNING TO SCHOOL AFTER A SUICIDE ATTEMPT

Students who have felt so helpless, hopeless, and worthless that they have made a suicide attempt have several strikes against them. The problems that led to the attempt have usually not vanished; instead they are augmented by having been hospitalized for making a suicide attempt. Peers may not be kind to someone returning to school after a psychiatric hospitalization. Even today there is an unfortunate stigma to having to go to a psychiatric hospital that is not attached to a stay in a drug or alcohol rehabilitation center.

Unfortunately, this negativity may not be limited to the student population. Insensitive and unthinking faculty and staff may also hold antiquated views about mental health treatment that lead to an unwelcoming climate for the returning student.

This section will review interventions that can assist in a student's positive reintegration into school after such a hospital stay. It will provide guidelines for faculty and staff and give examples of interventions that schools can implement to ease a student's transition back to a productive academic life.

## A STUDENT WHO RECENTLY ATTEMPTED SUICIDE IS RETURNING TO SCHOOL. HOW CAN I HELP BOTH THE STUDENT AND THE STAFF SO THAT HIS RETURN IS AS SMOOTH AS POSSIBLE?

Returning to school after any traumatic absence is daunting for students, but returning to school after a suicide attempt is especially difficult, particularly if "everyone knows" or if the student perceives that everyone knows. Perhaps the most important thing is to give the student as much control over the situation as possible. As Brian's example (on page 150) demonstrates, meeting with the student before the return, collaboratively planning what he or she does and doesn't want you to say and to whom, can empower the student and make returning a little easier. Actually scripting responses or doing a *behavioral rehearsal* can prepare the student for responding to situations that might lead to anxiety. Knowing, for example, that it's okay to answer intrusive questions as simply as "I don't really want to talk about it" gives the student permission to maintain as much privacy about the circumstances of his or her absence as needed.

Depending on the student's level of comfort, it can be helpful to get his or her permission (and if the student is under eighteen, the parents' permission) to brief teachers and relevant groups of students about how the student would like to be treated. It is also valuable for the school-based counselor to obtain consent to read discharge reports and recommendations and to consult with the outside therapist. This builds a safety net for the student.

## The Story of Brian

Brian, a seventeen-year-old high school junior and a gifted scholar-athlete, had made a suicide attempt the night before an all-state sports event and was immediately hospitalized in a psychiatric facility. The school superintendent, understanding that reintegrating a student into the school after a suicide attempt could be difficult, asked the school crisis counselor, a counseling school psychologist, to contact Brian's family and, with his parents' permission, arrange to visit him after his release from the hospital and before he returned to school.

The school psychologist called Brian's parents and arranged to visit him at home. She learned from his mother that Brian was already set up with an outside therapist as part of his discharge plan from the hospital. His parents agreed to let the school psychologist read the discharge report and also gave her permission to consult with the outside therapist.

During the visit to the house, Brian didn't talk much about his actual attempt. He did say that he had been feeling completely overwhelmed, trying to juggle his honors and advanced-placement classes with his social life and his athletics. Brian perceived his parents as having "impossible" expectations of him. He was supposed to be a straight-A student *and* a star athlete. When he had gotten injured "doing something dumb" right before the big all-state event, he had blamed himself and felt that he had really let down his whole team. It had "all just seemed too much."

Now Brian was worried about returning to school. Sitting with him on his front doorstep, the school psychologist helped him plan out in detail what he wanted her to tell his teachers and his teammates, essentially paving the way for him to return. He didn't want to be in the "spotlight," and he didn't want to be asked any questions. They discussed his concerns about feeling conspicuous and embarrassed, and they problem-solved together how to make returning to school "less worse." After Brian came back to school, he visited the school psychologist daily, then weekly, and then only occasionally, while continuing to participate in outside therapy.

## ARE THERE SOME STANDARD ACCOMMODATIONS FOR STUDENTS RETURNING AFTER A SUICIDE ATTEMPT?

There's really nothing standard about a student who has been hospitalized for a suicide attempt. The return to school requires individualized attention and regular follow-up that must be adjusted to the needs and abilities of each student. If the suicide attempt isn't public knowledge, not everyone in the school needs to know the details that surround the student's absence. Faculty and staff who have direct contact with the student, however, should be part of the safety net that monitors continuing risk. Provide them with instructions about the ways in which they may be most helpful to the returning student. These can include things like the following:

- Treat the student's return to the classroom as you would any absences related to other causes, such as illnesses. The consistency in responses will not garner unwanted special attention.

- Validate the student's return to school. You can suggest this same response to students who are unsure about what to say to the returning student.

   *"I'm glad to see you. We've missed you."*

- Respect the student's wishes for the way in which his or her absence is discussed. If the attempt is common knowledge, help the student prepare for the comments and questions from peers (or faculty and staff). If students are unaware of the attempt, assist the student in developing a short response to explain his or her absence. Being prepared for potentially embarrassing questions goes a long way in helping the student feel in control.

- Discuss missed class work and assignments and make arrangements for completion. If necessary, adjust immediate expectations.

   *"I know this has been an extremely difficult time for you. If you are having trouble concentrating on schoolwork, let's talk about a short-term strategy to take off some of the pressure. What do you think about a take-home assignment instead of having to turn in all your missed work?"*

- Monitor the student's academic performance and social interactions from a discreet distance. If you observe behavior that concerns you, then follow up with the student and his or her teachers.

- Take note of tardiness, absences, and requests to be excused during the course of a class. If they seem out of the ordinary, alert the appropriate staff resource person.

- Encourage the student to use the appropriate school resources for additional support.

- Provide regular feedback to school resource staff.

In some schools, what *may* be standard for returning students is laid out in policies and procedures that require a meeting at the school between the student, his or her parents, and selected school staff before the student is permitted to return. At this meeting, adjustments that might be necessary to the student's routine or class schedule might be discussed. Especially when students are in the process of adjusting to psychotropic medication, many schools find it helpful to implement a 504 plan (see description, below). This plan can specify in writing the ways in which the student's assignments, test taking, or schedule can be adjusted until the student is stabilized and able to participate fully again in school routine.

When the student does return to school, often the routine, predictability, and support available in the school can provide a sense of comfort to the student. Make sure, though, to check in with the returning student regularly to see how things are going.

*"At first I thought I was bugging Sammy by asking her to stop by and see me a couple of times a week when she returned to the school after her suicide attempt. So one day I apologized for being such a nudge and she burst into tears and told me how checking in with me was the best part of the day, next to having lunch with her friends."*

—STUDENT ASSISTANCE COUNSELOR

### What Is a 504 Plan?

The "504" in "504 plan" refers to Section 504 of the Rehabilitation Act and the Americans with Disabilities Act, which specifies that no one with a disability can be excluded from participating in federally funded programs or activities, including elementary, secondary, or postsecondary schooling. "Disability" in this context refers to a "physical or mental impairment that substantially limits one or more major life activities." A 504 plan spells out the modifications and accommodations that will be needed for these students to have an opportunity to perform at the same level as their peers.

**Guidelines for Reintegration for Faculty and Staff**

- Welcome the returning student privately
- Coach other classmates if necessary
- Treat the return to school like other excused absences
- Discuss missed assignments and make appropriate accommodations
- Observe and monitor
- Encourage use of additional school resources

The longer-term issues of reintegration after a suicide attempt require gentle and persistent attention to the academic performance and social behavior of the returning student. Some decline in performance might be expected in the aftermath of a psychiatric hospitalization, but the accommodations made to academic expectations should generally only be used on a short-term basis. Students who have had their academic standards excused for longer periods of time sometimes report thinking teachers "feel sorry" for them when they don't require them to work competitively with the rest of their class. Students who continue to have difficulty keeping up with academic expectations should be reevaluated by the school's resource team for a more comprehensive and long-term plan of support.

These guidelines are further discussed in the document Issues and Options Surrounding a Student's Return to School Following a Suicide-related Absence found on the CD-ROM.

**9-1**

# GIFTED STUDENTS

Inventories of suicide risk factors for youth don't necessarily mention the category of gifted youth, yet anyone acquainted with these students will attest to their social and emotional complexity. Although there is currently no evidence that gifted students are any less emotionally hardy than their peers, there is also no evidence that their suicide rate is lower than that of their peers. In fact, many studies of gifted adults have shown that there is a significantly higher incidence of mood disorders and suicide among gifted writers and visual artists (Neihart and Olenchak 2002, 168). Clearly, gifted adults were once gifted children.

What we do know for sure is that gifted youth face risks to their social and emotional development. For example, like all preteens and teens, gifted youth have a pressing need to belong, but often feel like they don't fit in. The reasons? Precisely the same talents and skills that make them unique. As experts in the field have wisely observed, "Privileges are the front side of giftedness, and discrimination is the back-side" (Thomas, Ray, and Moon 2007).

So even without epidemiological data pointing to their elevated risk for suicide or suicide attempts, there is certainly enough evidence about the challenges gifted students face to consider the potential risk factors posed by their giftedness and to consider how to intervene to moderate the negative effects in the school setting.

## WHY MIGHT GIFTED STUDENTS BE AT HIGHER RISK FOR SUICIDE?

If we look at the more common traits shared by gifted children, we can understand how these traits may also place them at an elevated suicide risk. It's important to note, though, that this represents an extremely abbreviated list of the characteristics of gifted children and is not meant to be either comprehensive or exhaustive. It's designed to stimulate your thinking about the gifted students in your school and the ways in which their giftedness might sometimes be a burden rather than an asset.

Especially when they are young, gifted children experience asynchronous development, with very advanced skills in some areas and less advanced skills in others. Their social-emotional skills, for example, may not develop at the same rate as their intellectual, musical, verbal, or mathematical skills. Some gifted students have the intelligence of an adult and the emotional capacity of a child, all in a child's body. Those gifted young people who are also socially aware may be acutely conscious of how different they are. Depending on the school culture (whether it is "cool to be smart"), they may feel that they have to put on an act, denying who they really are and what they care about to try to fit in. Some gifted students hide their grades and limit the vocabulary they use with other students. On the other hand, academically gifted students who are socially "clueless" may become targets of persistent bullying.

Asynchronous development has also been proposed as a risk factor for depression in gifted children. Being developmentally so different from the norm may produce additional stress and social isolation. Since peers normally turn to each other for support, gifted children may not receive the kind of emotional support that is crucial for social development, especially as they enter middle school.

Gifted youth also tend to be highly sensitive and emotionally intense. They may have precocious concerns about causes that their peers are unaware of and may be seen as "weird" because of their passionate interests and beliefs. This problem may be exacerbated by media depictions of gifted youth as geeks and oddballs.

## The Story of Elisabeth

Elisabeth was an extraordinary young woman. From an early age, we could tell that she was extremely gifted, creative, and compassionate, and she displayed a more sophisticated sense of humor than her peers. These are coveted traits. However, what often appears to be a blessing can sometimes result in being a curse.

Elisabeth could be described with one word: intense. When she was happy, she was very, very happy. When she was sad, it was horrible. Elisabeth's early years of development, until junior high school, had been easy for her. She had excelled in activities she participated in and made straight A's, effortlessly.

It was during the seventh-grade year that Elisabeth's problems with depression appeared from nowhere like a fog. She was no longer the smartest girl in the class or the fastest girl on the cross country team. How could this be? She knew she was gifted and knew the expectations that accompanied that label.

I watched as the pervasiveness of depression overtook her life. We sought medical and psychological treatment, which seemed to help for a while. However, the more Elisabeth viewed the injustices of the world, struggled with perfectionism, the more she felt she was not living up to the expectations she felt were placed on her by herself and others. These feelings caused a deeper descent into the fog.

During her eighth- and ninth-grade years, the fog somewhat lifted and Elisabeth seemed to enjoy life again. She began to channel her creativity and sense of humor into writing scripts and producing short videos, showcasing her friends and herself. It appeared that she was slowly regaining her love for life. However, the reprieve was short-lived. On June 13, 2006, after a weekend of fun with a childhood friend and family members, Elisabeth took her life.

After Elisabeth's death, it became clear to me that there is a myth regarding giftedness. People believe that gifted individuals have no problems. Elisabeth's life dispelled that myth. At that time, I realized how the intense affective characteristics of gifted individuals put them at risk for mental illness, as well as suicide.

—*Elisabeth's Mother*

Their emotional intensity may also make it difficult for them to engage in small talk with their peers. As one thirteen-year-old girl explained the reason for her social isolation: "I'm too mature for the kids in my grade. I don't want to talk about stupid stuff all the time. I'd rather talk with my teachers."

On the other hand, sensitivity can contribute to high levels of empathic understanding of peers. Connor, a fourteen-year-old, complained that "I can never get my homework done. Kids are always texting me with their problems 'cause I'm good at helping them figure out what to do."

Gifted students also tend to be highly perfectionistic, holding very high standards for themselves and others. One of the consequences of this perfectionism in an academic setting may be a social-intellectual imbalance. For example, gifted students may set high personal standards in areas where performance can be measured—like academic work—to the exclusion of social relationships that are both not measurable and based on friendship equity. The consequence, again, may be social isolation.

*"Katy was a gifted sophomore who excelled in academics but was pretty miserable in her personal relationships. She limited extracurricular activities so she had ample time to study and, while pleasant with her peers, didn't cultivate friendships because she 'needed to focus my time to get into a good college.' Any grade less than an A+ sent her into a panic. Her downfall was a group project in her honors history class. She came to the counselor complaining that one student was 'not pulling his weight' and the teacher refused to do anything about it. She had no idea what to do about it. When she got a grade of B+, she went home that night and took an overdose of Tylenol."*

—STUDENT ASSISTANCE COUNSELOR

Gifted students are also known to complain about the perceptions others hold of their giftedness. One sixteen-year-old student reported that she only feels appreciated for performing well. "The only reason anybody in the school knows who I am is because I win all these academic awards," she lamented. "Nobody wants to know anything else about me. The only time kids talk to me is to ask me about homework."

These perceptions about their intelligence can also compromise their ability to get emotional support when they honestly feel challenged.

> ## The Story of Sam
>
> Sam loved to play music, sing, and write poetry. He had zero interest in team sports, which set him apart from most of the other boys at his high school. Sam had started to become despondent. He told his mother, "I'm so lonely. I have no real friends." When she mentioned all the students he regularly spent time with, he responded, "They may like me, but there is no one I can relate to. No one actually gets me."
>
> One day Sam locked himself in his room and refused to come out. His worried mother, pleading through the door, asked him what she could do to help—change his school, move to a different neighborhood. No response. He finally said very quietly, "There's only one thing you can do. I don't want to be smart anymore."
>
> Sam became more and more depressed. After the suicide of a boy with whom he sang in the school choir, Sam finally confided to his mother that he, too, had been feeling suicidal.

*"I may be good at most of my subjects, but I hate chemistry and it's really hard for me. But if I complain that I don't know something or I'm afraid I might fail a test, my friends just say 'Blah, blah' and don't listen. And when I study really hard and do okay, they tell me like 'Yeah, of course you got an A. You always do.' But I listen to them when they get worried about grades so it's really unfair and makes me mad."*

—JOCELYN, AGE SEVENTEEN

Another unique capacity of gifted students is their ability to feel "existential dread," the feeling that may accompany pondering the unanswerable questions about the meaning (or meaninglessness) of life, death, and one's role in the universe. Gifted students may experience this feeling at an age when their peers are thinking about what to do on the weekend. Unfortunately, these musings can lead to depression caused by pessimistic perceptions of these basic issues of existence. Many gifted youth are burdened with the weight of such profound questions, and because they are so young, they lack the experience and perspective of age that can protect them from ensuing depression.

*"I got to the point where I just couldn't bear the inanity of my classmates. The biggest disappointment in their lives was that we hadn't won the all-state football championship. Who cares about football? I certainly don't."*

—DEVLIN, FIFTEEN YEARS OLD

## SOUNDS LIKE IT CAN BE REALLY HARD TO BE A GIFTED KID! ARE THERE ALSO SOME THINGS THAT ARE REALLY POSITIVE?

Looking at risk factors for suicide must always be balanced by considering those protective factors that serve as buffers against stress. For gifted youth, the protections against suicide may come from the same factors that reflect their overall giftedness: high intelligence, problem-solving ability, and the capacity to identify and interact with trusted adults. Most importantly, we know that strong social connections like those advocated in the *Lifelines* competent school model—in which everyone in the school community is concerned about each other's welfare—create a climate that fosters resiliency in all its members.

## SO WHAT'S MY TAKE-AWAY AS A SCHOOL COUNSELOR?

In much the same way that school counselors can help other students, they can help gifted students by being accepting and supportive and by providing a place where students can discuss their feelings and concerns. Additionally, it may be especially important for gifted students to have a trusted adult with whom they can discuss their passion about issues and with whom they can use their more mature vocabulary. The school counselor can also help gifted students grapple with their existential concerns and offer an adult perspective. Of course, the counselor must be alert to signs that either social difficulties, existential concerns, or perfectionism have triggered depression or anxiety and must be prepared to make an appropriate referral to community resources.

## STUDENTS WHO ARE BULLIED

The media has done a good job of bringing the topic of bullying into the national conversation. However, media reports tend to overstate and neglect the reality that the large percentage of students who are bullied make adaptive choices in response to the bullying situation. Bullying is worthy of special discussion because it is currently surrounded by a lot of conjecture and misinformation. In addition, it is one of the few risk factors for suicide that is *intentional* and *external* to an individual. So it also presents clear and unique opportunities for prevention.

## The Story of Thomas

Thomas was in the fifth grade when his parents first suspected that something was wrong. During his earliest years in elementary school, he'd been a reasonably popular kid, invited to the birthday parties of his classmates and busy with community activities like recreational sports teams. His schoolwork had been fine, although he'd never lived up to his academic potential, content to bring home B's when, as his mother explained, "With a little effort, he clearly could have done A work."

As he entered fifth grade, however, his social invitations began to drop off. Instead of a pickup basketball game in the neighborhood after school, he'd be home at his computer playing games. He started to put on weight as he exercised less and began to sneak cookies and candy into his room for snacks. His once agreeable mood began to sour, but his parents just chalked it up to the beginning of puberty. Despite being at home almost all the time now, he put even less effort into his schoolwork. He explained that his sliding grades were because "I have bad teachers." His worried parents spoke to his teachers who also had noticed the changes in his behavior, adding, "Thomas doesn't seem to have any friends."

One day, shortly after Thomas got home from school, his father asked Thomas to go out and check the mail. Remembering he had something else to tell his son, Thomas's father followed Thomas out the front door and was startled to see neighborhood kids walking down the street, throwing stones at his son. Thomas's father interrupted the kids who scattered in ten different directions.

When Thomas came in, he admitted to his father that he had been bullied for several months. "They call me the Dough-Boy because I'm fat and white," he cried. When asked why he hadn't told anyone, Thomas stated that he was afraid it would just get worse. He admitted to his father that some days it was so bad that he didn't want to go to school and that he had thought about running away or even killing himself. "Then it would be over," he said.

## EVERYONE IS TALKING ABOUT BULLYING, BUT THEY DON'T ALL SEEM TO MEAN THE SAME THING. WHAT IS BULLYING, ANYWAY?

While the word "bullying" seems to have become commonplace in American vocabulary today, it is important to define it in a more specific, research-based context. According to Dan Olweus, a pioneer in bullying prevention, bullying is aggressive behavior that is intended to cause harm or distress, occurs repeatedly over time, and occurs in a context in which there is an imbalance of power (Olweus 1993).

Bullying is sometimes described as "Double IR," referring to

- *Imbalance* of power

- *Intentional* acts

- *Repeated* over time

For example, in the story of Thomas, we can see the power imbalance in the number of neighborhood kids who have ganged up against him, the intentionality of their name calling, and the fact that these behaviors have been going on for at least several months.

Bullying does present itself in many different behaviors. Despite the different mediums of bullying, the overall definition remains the same. Bullying can be physical or verbal, direct (face to face) or indirect (social isolation or intentional exclusion). Cyberbullying, a relatively new form of indirect bullying, involves the use of technological devices such as cell phones and the Internet for targeting people. An especially insidious aspect of cyberbullying is that victims can be bullied twenty-four hours a day, seven days a week, by faceless, nameless tormenters who cannot even see the pain they are inflicting.

## I THOUGHT BULLYING WAS JUST A NORMAL PART OF GROWING UP. WHAT'S THE BIG DEAL?

According to Pamela Orpinas and Andy Horne, two well-known researchers and practitioners in the field of bullying prevention:

> Suicide and homicide are relatively rare consequences of bullying, but they highlight the reality that bullying may be followed by tragic events . . . Recently the U.S. Secret Service and the U.S. Department of Education examined characteristics of children who have been the perpetrators of school shootings. They found that almost three-fourths of the school shooting incidents by students against other students had in common the acting out of anger or revenge for having been the victims of bullying at school (Orpinas and Horne 2006, 31).

Research and experience have shown that bullied children and teens can suffer from significant mental health problems. Victims of bullying have been shown to display higher levels of social isolation, depression, and anxiety, especially among girls and bully-victims (those who are bullied and, in turn, bully others). There is also evidence of increased self-harm behaviors (such as cutting) and suicidal ideation among victims of bullying. Studies have demonstrated that being bullied makes a unique contribution to mental health problems. Bullying victimization in childhood can lead to an exacerbation of mental health problems in late childhood or adolescence, especially when mental health problems existed prior to the bullying victimization experience. Being bullied in childhood predicts suicide attempts up to the age of twenty-five among females, over and above the risk of suicide that is related to symptoms of conduct problems and depression that may have been present in childhood (Arsenealt, Bowes, and Shakoor 2010).

Cyberbullying has also been linked to suicide risk. In 2007, a random sample of almost two thousand middle-schoolers from one of the largest school districts in the United States completed a survey of Internet use and experiences. Students who experienced either traditional bullying or cyberbullying, as either an offender or a victim, had more suicidal thoughts and were more likely to attempt suicide than those who had not experienced these forms of peer aggression. Also, having been a victim of bullying was more strongly related to suicidal thoughts and behaviors than having bullied others (Hindujua and Patchin 2010).

Bullying peaks in middle childhood and decreases over the high school years (Finkelhor et al. 2009). This comes as no surprise to anyone who has experience with middle school students. The intensity of their peer attachments and their often desperate need to belong to a group can breed a climate of insiders and outsiders; anything that brands a student as "different" can mark that child as a potential victim. As students mature, they are less preoccupied with the differences in others and more concerned with themselves, so bullying behavior declines. That's not to say, however, that it disappears.

## HOW MANY STUDENTS ARE ACTUALLY AFFECTED BY BULLYING?

There have been many studies that have examined the numbers of students who have bullied or have experienced bully victimization. According to statistics reported by ABC News, nearly 30 percent of students are directly involved as either perpetrators of bullying or victims of bullying. As a result, up to 160,000 American children miss school every day because of their fear of being bullied.

Some studies have tried to break out the prevalence rates of specific types of bullying. It appears that verbal bullying (53.6 percent) and social or relational bullying

(51.4 percent) are the most prevalent types of bullying behaviors. Physical bullying happens least often at about 20 percent of the time. In terms of cyberbullying, the statistics are even more sobering. Statistics offered on www.bullyingstatistics.org state that more than 50 percent of kids report having said or being told mean or hurtful things online. Forty-two percent of kids report they have been "bullied" while online, with one in four reporting it happening more than once. Thirty-five percent of kids have been threatened online, with one in five reporting this happening more than once.

The most common methods of cyberbullying include the following:

- sending mean messages or threats to a person's e-mail account or cell phone

- spreading rumors online or through texts

- posting hurtful or threatening messages on social networking sites or Web pages

- stealing a person's account information to break into the account and send damaging messages

- pretending to be someone else online to hurt another person

- taking unflattering pictures of a person and spreading them through cell phones or the Internet

- "sexting" or circulating sexually suggestive pictures or messages about a person

Boys and girls are usually typically involved in different types of bullying experiences. Boys are more involved in physical bullying and verbal bullying, whereas girls are more involved in relational bullying. Boys are also more likely to cyberbully others, whereas girls are more likely to be cyber victims.

The good news is that there are protective factors against bullying and bully victimization. Support—both parental and peer—seems to make a difference. Higher parental support has been associated with less involvement with bullying regardless of the forms and classifications of bullying. Having more friends was associated with bullying others more, and being victimized less, for physical, verbal, and relational bullying but was not associated with cyberbullying (Wang, Iannotti, and Nansel 2009).

## ARE KIDS WHO DON'T BULLY OTHERS AND AREN'T BULLIED BY OTHERS STILL AFFECTED BY BULLYING?

Unfortunately, yes. Students who are neither bullied nor bully others may still be negatively affected by bullying. Bullying usually takes place in the presence of other peers. Many students either just watch or even instigate the aggression, without reporting the situation to an adult or intervening to help the target child. These children are called bystanders. According to research cited by Orpinas and Horne (2006), bystanders who witness a bullying incident may feel helpless or even guilty for not doing anything to stop it, thus increasing their risk for mental health problems.

## WON'T STUDENTS TELL SOMEONE AT SCHOOL IF THEY ARE BEING BULLIED?

Unfortunately, as shown in one study, only about a third of victims notify a teacher or another adult about it. In terms of cyberbullying, making mean, hurtful comments and spreading rumors seem to be most common. And, again, 58 percent of youth report that they did not tell their parents or an adult about something mean or hurtful that happened to them online.

## WHAT ARE POSSIBLE SIGNS THAT A STUDENT IS BEING BULLIED?

The following list suggests possible warning signs of bullying-victimization. The student

- returns home from school with torn, damaged, or missing articles of clothing, books, or belongings
- has unexplained cuts, bruises, and/or scratches
- has few, if any, friends
- appears afraid of going to school
- has lost interest in schoolwork
- complains of headaches or stomachaches
- has trouble sleeping and/or has frequent nightmares
- appears sad, depressed, or moody
- appears anxious and/or has poor self-esteem
- is quiet, sensitive, and passive

(Olweus, Limber, and Mihalic 1999)

## THE MEDIA REPORT STORIES ABOUT TEENS THAT TAKE THEIR LIVES AFTER HAVING BEEN BULLIED. IS THIS SOMETHING NEW?

In a recent interview, Susan Swearer, a national expert on bullying prevention from the University of Nebraska, responded to this very question:

> "The media are reporting cases where students commit suicide as a result of being bullied because these cases are so tragic and in some cases have resulted in lawsuits against the bullies and the schools. We should remember that Dr. Dan Olweus, the Norwegian researcher who started studying bullying in the early 1980s, did so partly as a result of three boys, ages ten to fourteen, who committed suicide in 1982 as a result of being bullied. Sadly, this is not a 'new' problem" (Swearer 2010).

*"When I saw the cover of People magazine making a connection between a young girl being bullied and her death by suicide, I knew that the young people in my classes would see that cover too and begin to link being bullied with making a suicide attempt. So I made sure when we talked about current events to discuss this article and remind students that there are so many other ways to deal with being bullied, including letting a trusted adult know about what's going on. The discussion with this sixth-grade class went so well that we expanded it to another class period to talk about all the other things this girl in the magazine could have done instead of taking her own life."*

*—SIXTH-GRADE HISTORY TEACHER*

The small number of research studies examining the links between bullying and suicide have shown that the teens who complete suicide after being bullied also have other serious suicide risk factors. The "overlap theory of risk factors," described in detail in chapter 4, certainly reflects this finding. So it's important to be alert to the reality of pre-existing risk factors when you're considering recommendations to the family of a student who may be a victim of bullying. The bullying incident is significant, however; in it may be the final straw or the triggering event that pushes an already vulnerable student to attempt suicide.

*"Harlan, the youngest of six siblings, had been a troubled kid for most of his school career. He was the class clown, his grades were poor, and he struggled to keep up with his sixth-grade classmates. He was absent a lot, but his parents seemed unconcerned when school staff raised questions about his poor performance in school and missed assignments. One day, Harlan took his older sister's cell phone and began to 'prank' call some of her friends, leaving inappropriate text messages, which he showed to his classmates. His classmates informed his teachers and school authorities notified Harlan's parents. After that, classmates would leave notes for Harlan, mimicking the content of his cell phone texts; at home, his sister's friends did the same thing. Three weeks later, Harlan took his life."*

—*SCHOOL SOCIAL WORKER*

Here's another important concern to put on your radar: media coverage of suicide deaths related to bullying may, in fact, exaggerate the connection between suicide and being bullied. By calling attention to the suicides of bullied teens and young adults, the reality that most youth who are bullied choose healthier solutions for dealing with being victimized is largely ignored. In the minds of vulnerable youth, suicide may become the one and only solution.

*"When I saw the cover of my mom's People magazine, there was a picture of a pretty girl with words like 'bullied to death' or something. I've been bullied, too, but haven't told anyone. That girl was so much cooler and prettier than I am and I thought if she had to die maybe I'd have to die too."*

—*SIXTH-GRADE GIRL*

Being alert to media coverage of suicide deaths that are attributed to bullying behaviors is a simple yet important suicide prevention technique that can be practiced in schools.

## HOW CAN I GET A STUDENT TO CONFIDE IN ME ABOUT BEING BULLIED?

In a perfect world, the culture of the school would support and encourage self-reporting and peer reporting of bullying. And while the number of bullying prevention initiatives in schools is certainly on the increase, many schools still have no formalized way for responding to bullied students. We have learned, though, whether a formal bullying prevention program exists in a school, students will confide in trusted adults under the following circumstances:

1. The adult is warm, encouraging, and supportive.

2. The adult is clear that this is one of the things that students sometimes talk about with him or her.

3. The student can be assured that his or her anonymity will be respected and that his or her report of bullying will be held strictly confidential.

4. The adult can ensure, and the student can believe, that reporting bullying in "our school" will actually improve the situation and not just make things worse.

## WHAT CAN SCHOOLS DO TO HELP?

Fortunately, researchers and practitioners have demonstrated that comprehensive school climate change/bullying prevention programs can greatly reduce the incidence of bullying in schools. These programs are discussed in detail in chapter 10. In the meantime, it can be helpful to keep the following facts in mind:

- Bullying is not a new problem; its roots lie in the group behavior of our species that singles out a scapegoat to victimize and abuse. It does not necessarily lead to suicide, but it may make youth who are already vulnerable more susceptible to suicide.

- Greater parental involvement is associated with less involvement in all forms of bullying.

- Prevention of bullying can be accomplished by strengthening the resiliency skills of students.

"Zero tolerance" policies toward bullying, in which children who bully others are suspended or expelled from school, are increasingly being implemented in school districts across the country. Although suspension and expulsion of students may be necessary to maintain public safety in a very small number of cases, these practices are not recommended as a broad-based bullying prevention or intervention policy. Threats of severe punishment like expulsion may discourage not only students but also adults from reporting bullying incidents. The most effective bullying prevention programs, as you will see in the next chapter, provide students with prosocial skills and role models, all in the context of a competent and compassionate school community. This approach also forms the foundation for the school's suicide prevention activities.

Schools can circulate some specific guidelines like these to help students deal with cyberbullying:

- Tell a trusted adult about the bullying, and keep telling until the adult takes action.

- Tell your school if the bullying is school-related. Most schools have a bullying solution in place.

- Don't open or read messages by the person who is cyberbullying you.

- Don't erase the messages—they may be needed to take action.

- If you are bullied through chat or instant messaging, then block the number.

- If you are threatened with harm, inform the local police.

Finally, as researchers concluded, a suicide prevention and intervention component should be an essential element within comprehensive bullying response programs (Hindujua and Patchin 2010).

**9-2**

See What Can Schools Do to Address Bullying? on the CD-ROM and chapter 10 for more information on bullying prevention and intervention.

## SEXUAL MINORITY STUDENTS

Sexual minority students are young people who identify as gay, lesbian, bisexual, transgender, or questioning. In research and practice, the terms "LGB," "LGBT," and "LGBTQ" (with the "Q" standing for both questioning and queer) are often used. The term "transgender," as you may know, means an individual who identifies with the gender opposite to his or her biological gender. Throughout this section we use LGB, LGBT, and LGBTQ depending on which groups were included in the studies referenced.

This section discusses specific risks for suicide that sexual minority students face. But first, it is important to note that students who are part of *any* oppressed minority may be vulnerable to depression, anxiety, and suicidal feelings, especially when multiple risk factors are present. In the National Longitudinal Study of Adolescent Health, "perceived student prejudice" was the only variable identified in the school as a risk factor for emotional distress and suicide (Benard and

Marshall). There is also an important link between bullying and bias. In a survey of teen health among sixth to twelfth graders, 50 percent of the students reported that they had experienced bias-based harassment based on race, ethnicity, gender, or perceived sexual orientation (Seattle Teen Health Survey 1999).

Take a look at the story of Eduardo, who not only was the sole Latino student and one of the few non-white students in his high school, he was also struggling with the realization that he was gay.

## The Story of Eduardo

"Eduardo, a high school senior, had made a disturbing entry in the daily journal he was keeping for his English class. His alert teacher read the words 'I don't deserve to be alive' and immediately referred him to me, the school-based crisis counselor. Over the next two hours, the young man, whose family had moved to the United States from South America and then abandoned him, poured out his story. Eduardo was the only Latino student in our very white, mostly affluent school district. Working and living at a hotel in town, he felt alone and isolated.

"The problem that he really needed to talk about, though, was that he had come to the realization that he was very attracted to other boys, although he had never had a relationship or acted on his feelings. 'In my country,' he said, 'I would be stoned to death for these feelings.' His relief at being listened to and accepted was palpable. He had been literally dying to talk to someone. After a little searching, I was able to find a therapist in a local mental health center who specialized in LGBT issues. Eduardo's outside therapist helped him connect with a support group for gay and lesbian youth in a nearby town; the group helped him feel much less alone. The therapist and I worked collaboratively with Eduardo for the rest of the school year until he graduated. (P. S. The school and his employer together threw him a graduation party.)"

—*School Psychologist*

## ARE LGBTQ STUDENTS AT A HIGHER RISK FOR SUICIDAL BEHAVIOR?

Several studies have demonstrated higher levels of self-reported suicidal ideation and attempts among LGBTQ adolescents compared to heterosexual adolescents. Studies (Russell and Joyner 2001; Suicide Prevention Resource Center 2008; Almeida et al. 2009) report that LGBT youth report suicidal ideation at rates one-and-a-half to two times the rates of non-LGBT youth. Rates of attempts are also significantly higher among LGBT youth with reports ranging from two-and-a-half to seven times more likely than for non-LGBT youth.

It should be noted that the studies discussed in this section refer to suicidal ideation and suicide attempts. Data collection regarding actual suicide completions is limited, as sexual orientation is not generally included on death reports and certificates.

## ARE THERE SPECIFIC RISK FACTORS FOR SEXUAL MINORITY STUDENTS?

Of course, sexual minority youth share many of the same risk factors as the general youth population. However, LGBT youth have more risk factors and often experience more severe risk factors. Exposure to suicide is an example of how risk factors might be more severe for sexual minority youth. LGBT youth tend to know more youth who have attempted or died by suicide.

Furthermore, while victimization exists indiscriminately, LGBT youth get victimized repeatedly, and sometimes severely, in different settings. There is not much research that includes transgender youth, but it is likely that they also experience rejection, discrimination, isolation, and victimization and lack many protective factors.

Some risk factors are specific to sexual minority youth and are called "gay-related stress." They include factors such as those related to coming out. Others are related to the kinds of stress minorities experience from social discrimination and stigma (Suicide Prevention Resource Center 2010). These risk factors may be related to increased depression among LGBTQ youth which, as we discussed in chapter 4, is significantly related to suicidal ideation, attempts, and completions.

As we can see, LGBTQ youth may have more risk factors for suicide. Unfortunately, given the potential bias against LGBTQ youth and the coming out process, these young individuals may also have fewer protective factors to buffer the risk for suicide. LGBTQ youth generally have fewer protective factors than their heterosexual peers, such as safe schools and supportive families.

## HOW COMMON IS "COMING OUT" IN HIGH SCHOOL?

*"I knew I was gay when I was in high school, but there was no way in the world I was going to come out. Interestingly enough, my parents were really supportive and I knew they suspected; my mom would leave books about sexual identity in conspicuous places in the house. No, it wasn't them; it was me. I was sure that no one in my conservative school would support me when it came down to it. So I had to pretend to be someone I wasn't and it was really, really hard and contributed, I think, to my depression."*

—ANDREW, TWENTY YEARS OLD

Many sexual minority students experience tremendous emotional stress before, during, and after the coming out process. Questioning students are dealing with confusing and contradictory internal feelings and reactions, as well as their fears of possible ridicule, rejection, and isolation from their friends, schoolmates, families, and even their faith communities. Even sexual minority youth who are more certain of their sexual orientation face many of the same issues.

The age at which a young person is identifiable as LGB, as well as the age of coming out, appears to be related to the risk of suicide attempts—the younger the student identifies as LGB, the higher the risk of suicide. In a 2005 study, researchers compared LGB students who had reported suicide attempts with LGB students who had not. Of those who had reported attempts, about half of the attempts were reportedly related to the youths' sexual orientation. Sexual-orientation-related attempts were associated with being identified as LGB, especially by parents. Gay-related suicide attempts, especially for males, were related to

- early openness about sexual orientation
- being considered gender atypical in childhood by parents
- parental efforts to discourage gender atypical behavior

(D'Augelli et al. 2005).

*"I was beaten as a child for being too effeminate. I was clinically depressed at the age of eight and have battled the thoughts of suicide as a young teenager. I have no connection with my family and I wish to exclude them from my life after graduation."*

—JOHN, SIXTEEN YEARS OLD

## WHAT ARE THE ROLES OF BULLYING, BIAS, AND HARASSMENT AS SUICIDE RISK FACTORS FOR LGBTQ YOUTH?

The most fortunate sexual minority youth experience relief and acceptance when they come out to friends or family members, while others suffer the very rejection and isolation they had feared. Like racial, ethnic, and religious minority youth, many LGBTQ students face oppression, bullying, harassment, victimization, and possible violence. All of these are environmental risk factors for suicidality. In the 2009 study discussed earlier, Almeida and associates concluded that it was *not having a minority sexual orientation itself* that elevated risk, but rather the *degree to which these young people experienced prejudice and discrimination*. Perceived discrimination accounted for increased depressive symptoms among LGBTQ males and females and accounted for an elevated risk of self-harm and suicidal ideation among LGBTQ males. Sexual minority adolescents are disproportionately subjected to violence and harassment at school and to physical and sexual abuse (Saewyc et al. 2009).

Turning again to the 2008 report by the Suicide Prevention Resource Center in a study of high school students, we learn these facts:

- LGBT youth were almost five times as likely as non-LGBT youth to have missed school because of fears about their safety, and they were more than four times as likely to have been threatened with a weapon on school property.

- In addition to outright victimization, many sexual minority students experience isolation, ostracism, and stressed relationships with other students and even with school staff, who may or may not be prepared or willing to intervene on their behalf if they are being bullied or harassed.

*"I consider myself one of the lucky ones. I have an older cousin who is openly gay and I remember thinking when I was about thirteen or so that he was paving the way for me."*

*—LEW, AGE SIXTEEN*

Youth who are questioning their sexual orientation are at a greater risk for bully victimization, which, as we've discussed, increases their suicide risk. A 2009 study (Birkett, Espelage, and Koenig) found that LGB and sexually questioning youth were more likely to report high levels of bullying and homophobic victimization. Students who were questioning their sexual orientation reported the most bullying, the most homophobic victimization, the most drug use, the most feelings of depression and suicidality, and more truancy compared with either heterosexual or LGB students.

## IF I THINK A STUDENT MAY BE STRUGGLING WITH A SEXUAL IDENTITY ISSUE, HOW DO I ASK ABOUT IT? *DO* I ASK ABOUT IT?

When students appear to talk "around" a problem or indicate that they have a problem they can't talk about, they are sometimes testing the waters, indirectly referring to an issue of sexual orientation or bullying or even abuse. In this event, clearly communicate that it would be okay to talk with you about almost anything (as long as you *genuinely* mean it!) and that, unless there is danger to self or others, you will keep what students tell you completely confidential. Try something like "Sometimes kids talk with me about all kinds of things, including their relationships or if they are wondering about their sexuality or if they have been hurt in some way." This kind of statement doesn't necessarily elicit instant disclosures, but it can plant the idea that you might be a safe person to talk to about something difficult. It is also important to lay the groundwork for conversations about sexual orientation by always being careful not to assume that any given student is necessarily heterosexual. So, for example, rather than asking a girl "So do you have a boyfriend?" ask instead "Is there someone special in your life right now?"

Finally, school-based adults who want to express nonverbally their willingness to be supportive to sexual minority (and all potentially vulnerable) students can also put a rainbow or Safe Space sticker (available from GLSEN, the Gay, Lesbian and Straight Education Network) on their doors. In this way, you can make sure that students know that you believe that everyone has the right to be safe and comfortable at school.

## ARE THERE STUDENTS WHO DON'T EVEN START QUESTIONING THEIR SEXUAL ORIENTATION UNTIL AFTER HIGH SCHOOL?

Anyone who has experience with adolescents can probably name youth who seemed to be gay, lesbian, or bisexual but acted in either heterosexual or asexual ways. Only they can tell us whether they are questioning their sexual identity. For some of these youth, this questioning may be taking place very privately; for others, this awakening may not take place for some time.

*"If you had asked me in high school if I were a lesbian, I would have denied it vehemently. Even though I had no sexual interest in boys and would often play the male role in my drama group plays, I refused to let myself consider this possibility. My group of friends never treated me any differently and I didn't really care what kids who didn't know me thought. It wasn't until college that I began to think about my sexuality in a more conscious way. I don't think I was mature enough to have that conversation with myself when I was younger."*

—STEPHANIE, TWENTY-FOUR YEARS OLD

The bottom line is that sexual identification is a very individual, unique process. Students deserve the freedom to pursue questions about sexual orientation at their own pace. If the school observes any type of discrimination, however, intervention is obviously required immediately to address the bullying or bias.

## SPECIAL EDUCATION STUDENTS

Some research suggests that youth with learning disabilities, reading problems, and attention deficit/hyperactivity disorder (ADHD) may be at higher risk for suicidal behaviors. For example, in the National Longitudinal Study of Adolescent Health discussed earlier, students with learning disabilities attempted suicide more often than youth without learning disabilities (Resnick et al. 1997). In a 2006 study (Daniel et al.), teens with poor reading ability were more likely to experience suicidal ideation or attempts and more likely to drop out of school than young people with normal reading skills. Suicidality and school dropout were also strongly associated with each other.

The major focus of most publications, however, is on the links between depression and suicide. They suggest that since the cognitive deficits and diminished problem solving symptomatic of depression are also observed in many students with special needs, there may be some connection between the two. Although this may be true, we can simply observe these special needs students in action to get a sense of what may place them at elevated risk for suicidality.

> ### The Story of Holly
>
> "Holly was a classified student in the sixth grade when she was referred to counseling after a brief psychiatric hospitalization for a suicide attempt. Large for her age, Holly also has a bad case of acne and was taunted by classmates who called her 'pizza face.' Challenged by learning difficulties to keep up with her classmates, Holly had begun to substitute 'might for right' and was increasingly aggressive to the students who performed better in class than she did. Even though she established good rapport with the school counselor, she rarely practiced the less aggressive coping strategies they discussed together. One day, after a verbal altercation with several girls, Holly was observed by a teacher tying the strap from her purse around her neck. When she was stopped and brought to the counselor, she explained that she was playing the 'choking game'—and intended to kill herself to get back at the girls who were fighting with her."
>
> —*Holly's Sixth-grade Teacher*

Holly's aggression and lack of social skills contributed to her estrangement and isolation from peers in that vulnerable middle school period when personal worth may be determined by how many friends a student has. Her use of the choking game, common among her age mates, was to the extreme; rather than seeing it as a way to increase euphoric feelings, Holly's intention was to strangle herself and die. (She did, in fact, attempt to choke herself again in the girl's room, where she was found unconscious by several peers.) Even before her suicide attempts and without making a definitive psychiatric diagnosis, Holly seemed to present with a multitude of observable risk factors that would signal a specific suicide risk assessment by her counselor.

## ARE SPECIAL EDUCATION STUDENTS BULLIED MORE OFTEN THAN THEIR GENERAL EDUCATION PEERS?

Although there is very little documentation in academic studies, the simple answer appears to be yes. A 2010 analysis of the available data indicated that students with disabilities are victimized more often than students without disabilities (Rose, Monda-Amaya, and Espelage). A majority of the reviewed studies documented increased verbal abuse (including name calling, mimicking characteristics related to the disability, teasing), social exclusion, and physical aggression, as compared to nondisabled students. In one study, students with mild to moderate learning disabilities were two to three times more likely to be victimized than nondisabled peers. Furthermore, students with observable disabilities (physical disabilities, hearing impairments) were even more likely to be victimized. Finally, students in special classes or separate schools were victimized more often than students with disabilities in inclusive settings.

Some special education students were also found to be more likely to bully others. Overall, students with high-incidence disabilities (learning disabilities, emotional or behavioral disabilities) bullied others about twice as often as students without disabilities. In one study, girls with learning disabilities were up to ten times more likely to bully than were other female students. On the other hand, students with language impairments, psychiatric disorders, dyslexia, paralysis, or severe cognitive disabilities were much less likely to bully than either students with high-incidence disabilities or their general education peers.

Just as with other students who bully, students with disabilities may bully others for a variety of reasons. Some students are finally reacting to prolonged victimization; others may have an overall deficit of social-emotional skills (assertiveness, self-control, reading social communication); still others may have learned the behavior at home or in other social situations.

As mentioned earlier, students who are bully-victims may be especially at risk for suicidal behavior.

## WHAT SHOULD SCHOOLS DO TO HELP STUDENTS WITH DISABILITIES WHO ARE AT RISK FOR SUICIDE?

Again, very few studies address specific intervention approaches for at-risk special education students. In reaching out to these students, allow the principles of the competent school community to guide you. When the culture of the school reflects a genuine concern for all members and everyone knows where and how to access help for anyone in need, special interventions may not be necessary.

## LET'S REVIEW

Although a variety of circumstances can place students at an elevated risk for suicide, this chapter has focused on very specific groups of students whose school careers are often filled with additional stressors. One of the first things you as a school resource staff member can do to provide these students with the safety of a supportive school climate is to examine any personal attitudes, values, and prejudices that might affect your ability to offer these youth your nonjudgmental support. You can also keep abreast of emerging research as well as new resources for these potentially at-risk kids. Finally, work to make your school an inclusive, compassionate community where all students are accepted, regardless of their differences.

**IN YOUR**
## Experience . . .

- What incidents of bullying have you observed in your school? How were they handled?

- Think about students in these special populations that you've counseled. What made helping them difficult for you? What could you have done differently that might have positively affected the outcome?

- What information in this chapter made you think differently about these special groups of students?

## RESOURCES

### *Gifted Students*

Ellsworth, J. "Adolescence and Gifted: Addressing Existential Dread," 2003. Accessed at Supporting Emotional Needs of the Gifted, www.sengifted.org.

Neihart, M. "Risk and Resilience in Gifted Children: A Conceptual Framework." In *The Social and Emotional Development of Gifted Children*, edited by M. Neihart, S. Reis, N. M. Robinson, and S. M. Moon, 113–24. Waco, TX: Prufrock Press, 2002.

Plucker, J. A., and J. J. Levy. "The Downside of Being Talented." *American Psychologist* 56 (2001): 75–76.

Reis, G. M., and J. S. Renuzzi. "Current Research on the Social and Emotional Development of Gifted and Talented Students: Good News and Future Possibilities." *Psychology in the Schools* 41, no. 1 (2004): 119–30.

Robinson, N. M. "Introduction." In *The Social and Emotional Development of Gifted Children,* edited by M. Neihart, S. Reis, N. M. Robinson, and S. M. Moon. Waco, TX: Prufrock Press, 2002.

Webb, J. T. "Existential Depression in Gifted Individuals," 2002. Accessed at Supporting Emotional Needs of the Gifted, www.sengifted.org.

### Students Who Are Bullied

Davis, S., and C. Nixon. Youth Voice Project, 2010. See www.youthvoiceproject .com.

Goldbaum, S., W. M. Craig, D. Pepler, and J. Connolly. "Developmental Trajectories of Victimization: Identifying Risk and Protective Factors." *Journal of Applied School Psychology* 19 (2003): 138–56.

Kaltiala-Heino, R., M. Rimpela, M. Marttunen, A. Rimpela, and P. Rantanen. "Bullying, Depression, and Suicidal Ideation in Finnish Adolescents: School Survey." *British Medical Journal* 319 (1999): 348–51.

Nansel, T., M. Overpeck, R. S. Pilla, W. J. Ruan, B. Simmons-Morton, and P. Schmidt. "Bullying Behaviors among U.S. Youth." *Journal of American Medical Association* 285 (2001): 2094–2100.

### Special Education Students

G.A.S.P: Games Adolescents Shouldn't Play (information on The Choking Game). See www.gaspinfo.com.

Guetzloe, E. C. *Depression and Suicide: Special Education Students at Risk.* Reston, VA: Council for Exceptional Children, 1991.

Guetzloe, E. C. *Suicide and the Exceptional Child.* ERIC EC Digest #E508, November 1991. See www.parentpals.com/gossamer/pages/Detailed/609 .html.

## HANDOUTS

9-1: Issues and Options Surrounding a Student's Return to School Following a Suicide-related Absence

9-2: What Can Schools Do to Address Bullying?

# Chapter 10

# Enhancing Protective Factors and Building Resilience

*"Our school was in the unfortunate position of experiencing the suicide of several students in a relatively short period of time. We did everything we needed to do to identify other students who might be at risk, provided training and support to faculty and staff, but the climate in the school seemed changed. We just couldn't seem to recover the energy and optimism that has always characterized our student body, even in the most difficult of times. This went on for at least an academic year. Then one of our coaches got inspired; he decided to hold a Life Is Good day, with inspirational speakers, community involvement—he even contacted the company that makes Life Is Good T-shirts and got them to donate one for each student. What a difference that day made! The school seemed to turn around, and the program was so well received by faculty and staff it has become one of our annual assemblies."*

*—SCHOOL SUPERINTENDENT*

As noted in the beginning of this manual, intervention for suicide risk in the school setting has two distinct yet related aspects: (1) recognizing and assessing for suicide risk and (2) enhancing protective factors and building resilience. The preceding chapters have focused on students who are already feeling suicidal. We have discussed risk factors for suicide, outlined strategies for meeting with and referring at-risk students and their families, and described the special problems of potentially high-risk populations. This chapter will provide several examples of programs and practices that help foster protective factors for our students and that help create caring and competent school communities.

By the end of this chapter, you will be able to

- describe factors that can increase the resilience of students and protect against some types of suicide risk

- understand the importance of school connectedness

- recognize characteristics of programs that can support and encourage student resilience

## I'VE HEARD A LOT ABOUT THE RISK FACTORS FOR SUICIDE ATTEMPTS. WHAT ARE "PROTECTIVE FACTORS," AND DO THEY HELP PROTECT AGAINST YOUTH SUICIDE?

Fortunately, the answer is YES! Researchers and practitioners have been turning their attention to exactly this question. They have learned that personal qualities, relationships, and opportunities can protect young people, even those with serious risk factors, and can promote resilience, confidence, and competence. These protective factors arise from both individual attributes and social environments, including families, friends, schools, and communities. Bonnie Benard (1991), a pioneer in the study of resilience, has grouped these protective factors into three major categories:

1. Caring and supportive relationships

2. Positive and high expectations

3. Opportunities for meaningful participation

You may be familiar with the concept of developmental assets, which is another name given to protective factors. The National Longitudinal Study of Adolescent Health identified forty developmental assets, but the finding that stood out consistently was this: in their families, schools, and communities, young people need to feel connected and cared about (Resnick et al. 1997). According to researchers who analyzed the results of the study (Borowsky, Ireland, and Resnick 2001), the presence of just three protective factors greatly reduces the risk of a suicide attempt for each gender and all racial and ethnic groups, including youth with identified risk factors.

Here's what else their study showed:

Parent-family connectedness and perceived school connectedness were protective against every health risk behavior measure except history of pregnancy.

Finally, let's take a look at the protective factors identified by the Suicide Prevention Resource Center in its review of relevant research (2008):

- family connectedness
- family acceptance
- safe schools
- caring adult
- high self-esteem
- positive role models

As you can see, there is overlap and agreement on the characteristics, events, circumstances, and life experiences that can protect youth from the risk of harmful behaviors such as suicide attempts.

## AS SCHOOL STAFF WE CLEARLY CAN'T IMPACT HOW CONNECTED STUDENTS FEEL TO THEIR FAMILIES, OR WHETHER THEIR FAMILIES ACCEPT THEM. WHAT CAN WE DO ABOUT THE OTHER PROTECTIVE FACTORS?

School can be an oasis of stability for students who have serious problems at home.

> "School has always been my safe place, as home has served as my hell. An alcoholic stepdad would ensure that the screams throughout the night would keep me frozen in fear." (Alisa, age fifteen)

> "I wouldn't say my house was a 'crazy place.' It was just noisy and loud and, as the oldest of seven children, I found it could be really hard to get anyone to listen to me. But when I went to school, between my friends and my coach and this great history teacher, I always felt important and like people cared about me." (Lester, age seventeen)

> "I really like to go to school. Since my mom died, my dad is real sad and not very fun. But my teacher is nice and asks me every day how I'm doing." (Christine, age eight)

*Lifelines: A Suicide Prevention Program*, which is the first part of the *Lifelines* series, focuses on increasing protective factors within the school. It approaches the school from the perspective of the competent community, which has been mentioned so often in this manual. The approach begins at the top, reinforcing the administrative infrastructure to make sure there are board-approved policies and procedures that support suicide prevention, intervention, and postvention. When these are in place, and there is commitment from school leaders, a faculty/staff training out-lines the critical, but limited, role school staff members play in the identification of potentially at-risk students and their referral to school resources for assessment and intervention (that's where this intervention manual comes in!). Parents are another key part of the foundation of the competent community. They receive accurate information to help them understand the realities of youth suicide and to reinforce the importance of recognizing the signs of risk in their children and pursuing an evaluation by a mental health professional.

Finally, when all these components are in place to create a comprehensive safety net for students, the curriculum is introduced. Designed for students in middle school and high school, the content focuses on recognizing signs of suicide risk in oneself or others, learning how to talk about what's been observed, and reaching out to a trusted adult for help. The results are a "double win." Students become more connected to school through the establishment of a shared culture that advocates suicide prevention. Additionally, students' feelings of personal efficacy increase because they now have a clear plan for what to do when a friend is in need.

Evaluation of the *Lifelines* curriculum has shown significant gains in relevant knowledge about suicide and significantly more positive attitudes toward help-seeking and intervening with potentially suicidal peers. Student reactions to the curriculum have been positive, and students emphasize the utility of the classes for helping them with friends' problems. Students also express more confidence in the school response capability, recognizing that school staff members have been trained to respond to at-risk students (Kalafat and Ryerson 1999).

## PEER RESOURCE PROGRAMS

Students themselves may be the most underutilized resource for implementing positive change in schools. Bonnie Benard, mentioned earlier as a pioneer in the field of youth resilience, has identified what she calls a "critical need for the prevention and education fields to change the framework from which they often view youth—to see children and youth not as problems which need to be fixed but as resources who can contribute to their families, schools, and communities" (Benard 2004, 9). Peer resource programs—which include peer leadership, peer education, peer tutoring, and peer mediation—are an important way for youth to provide service to other students and to become part of the solution.

To understand how important peer resource programs can be in the lives of their young members, read about Isabella:

> "I was brought to America to live with my mother, stepdad, and
> half-sisters when I was twelve years old. My mother struggles

*Lifelines: A Suicide Prevention Program* is a comprehensive suicide prevention program that targets the entire school community, providing suicide awareness material for administrators, faculty and staff, parents, and students. It educates students on the facts about suicide and students' role in suicide prevention.

*Lifelines Postvention: Responding to Suicide and Other Traumatic Death* is a comprehensive, whole-school best-practices manual specifically designed for middle and high school communities. This unique program educates everyone in the school community on how to successfully address and respond to not only suicide, but any type of traumatic death that profoundly affects the school population.

with me being here and shows no interest in me as being a part of her family. Her brother sexually abused me and she refuses to acknowledge this, as if it was my fault or it never happened. I am overwhelmed with this every day . . . every day.

"It's hard to put into words exactly what 'peer' means to me. I am a part of the safest place I have ever known. I have learned to open both my mind and my heart, and now when I listen to people, I understand what they are feeling and not just what they're saying. The strength of my friendships and confidence in my convictions will remain with me always." (Isabella, age sixteen, peer mediator)

It's not only the peer participants who benefit when a school has a well-implemented peer resource program; the whole school community can receive a positive impact. Peer programs have been called the state-of-the-art approach for substance abuse prevention, HIV prevention, violence prevention, and other health-promoting interventions (Wyman et al. 2010; Johnson 1996).

Lifelines Intervention

· · · · · · · · · · · · · · · · · · · · · · · · · · · · · · · · · · · · · · · · · · · · · · · · · · · · · · · · · · · · · · · · · · · · · · · · · · · · · · · · · · ·

**184**

### *Why Do Students Need to Get Involved in Suicide Prevention? Isn't That an Adult Responsibility?*

Recent research on the effect of gatekeeper training has shown that adult training alone is unlikely to significantly increase our detection of and response to suicidal youth (Wyman et al. 2010). In the same study, students were surveyed about their willingness to seek adult help. Overall, the students reported that they were most likely to seek help through their peer friendships. Suicidal youth were the least likely to seek adult help.

Additionally, we have to face the fact that our students are *already involved* with suicidal peers. Here's what researchers found when they asked high school students about their knowledge and behavior regarding suicidal peers: more than two-thirds of the female students and almost half of the male students reported that they knew a teen who had attempted or completed suicide. Almost a third of them reported having actually talked with a peer who was definitely considering suicide (Kalafat and Elias 1992).

Here are some other important things we've learned from research and experience:

- Contact with helpful school adults can be a protective factor for troubled youth.

- School personnel are consistently among the *last* choices of adolescents for discussing personal concerns.

- Providing help to other students is also beneficial to the helpers in terms of shaping prosocial behaviors and developing social competencies.

- Disturbed (depressed, substance-abusing) youth prefer support from peers as opposed to adults more than their non-disturbed peers do.

- Some adolescents, particularly boys, do not respond to troubled peers in empathetic or helpful ways.

- Only 25 percent of peer confidants tell an adult about their troubled or suicidal peer.

(Kalafat 2003)

This research underscores that adolescents themselves are vitally important for the prevention of teen suicide and that, in particular, students need to be convinced to report at-risk peers to an adult. Until recently, though, there was no empirical evidence that trained peer leaders could participate meaningfully in youth suicide prevention programs. However, a National Peer Leadership Study has established the Sources of Strength program as the first suicide prevention program involving peer leaders to enhance protective factors associated with reducing suicide at the school population level.

Sources of Strength is a school-wide health promotion and suicide prevention program (Wyman et al. 2010). An important aspect is that it brings peer leaders and trained school adults together for added "prevention power." Peer leaders from diverse social groups, including at-risk students, are trained to conduct systematic suicide prevention messaging activities. These activities include peer-to-adult and peer-to-peer contacts, classroom presentations, and public service announcements. The program's overarching goal is to increase positive help-seeking behaviors among the general student population and to break the "code of silence" that can keep students from seeking adult help when they or their peers are in crisis. Peer leaders are trained to model help-seeking behaviors and encourage their friends to

- name and engage trusted adults

- create and reinforce an expectation that friends should ask adults for help for suicidal friends

- identify and use protective factors, or "Sources of Strength," including family support, positive friends, mentors, healthy activities, generosity, medical access, and mental health resources

By harnessing the power of peer group influence on adolescent norms and behaviors, the Sources of Strength program has been shown to enhance high school students' help-seeking and partnering with trusted adults to help peers who are in crisis. The 2008 research results (with six high schools, 177 peer leaders, and 4,300 students surveyed) showed a positive impact on both the trained peer leaders and the entire student population of the schools they served. Peer leaders showed an increase in their acceptance of help-seeking from and communication with adults. After the program, peer leaders were four times as likely to actually refer a suicidal peer for adult help. Also, help-seeking norms were affected across the entire student population, with the most positive impact being among students who identified themselves as suicidal and less connected than other students.

## BULLYING PREVENTION PROGRAMS

We saw in chapter 9 that severe bullying in school can lead to serious mental health problems for bully-victims, as well as for the targets. Conversely, we have just seen that school safety and school connectedness are protective factors for youth. So it stands to reason that effective programs for bullying prevention would address these two variables.

Lifelines Intervention
. . . . . . . . . . . . . . . . . . . . . . . . . . . . . . . . . . . . . . . . . . . . . . . . . . . . . . . . . . . . . . . . . . . . . . . . . . . . . . . . . . . . . . . . . . . . . .

**186**

Many recent program initiatives have sought to reduce bullying in schools. From the results of these programs, we have learned a great deal about what works, and what does not work, to make an impact on the problem of school bullying.

## What Has **Not** Worked?

- **Zero tolerance or "three strikes and you're out."** There is no evidence to date that these harsh disciplinary policies, which can lead to expulsion of students, actually reduce bullying. Moreover, these policies are reactionary rather than preventive in nature. The best discipline policies focus on finding solutions rather than merely punishing perpetrators (Orpinas and Horne 2006).

- **Group treatment for those who bully.** Increased contact with aggressive peers can lead to an escalation or reinforcement of bullying behavior (Orpinas and Horne 2006).

- **Mediation between bully and target.** Because of the imbalance of power, bullying situations are not normal peer conflicts that can be addressed through mediation (see Olweus Bullying Prevention website, Frequently Asked Questions, www.olweus.org).

- **Simple short-term solutions** (such as assemblies). An eye-opening assembly can inspire awareness and even short-term behavioral change; however, the effect dissipates and is soon forgotten. The only proven way to have an impact on bullying and improve school climate is through long-term, sustained efforts (Fleming and Towey 2002).

## What Has **Worked**?

Research has clearly shown that the key to preventing bullying and creating lasting, positive change in school climate is to get everyone in the school involved in a long-term effort to build a competent, caring school community. The *Olweus Bullying Prevention Program (OBPP)*, originally developed in Norway, is widely viewed as the "gold standard" in bullying prevention. A comprehensive, school-wide program designed for elementary, middle, or junior high schools, *OBPP* has been identified as one of only eleven national Blueprints for Violence Prevention by the Center for the Study and Prevention of Violence at the University of Colorado. The program aims to reduce and prevent bullying problems among school children and to improve peer relations at school. Studies have found that the schools implementing *OBPP* have reduced bullying among students, improved the social climate of classrooms, and reduced related antisocial behaviors, such as vandalism and truancy (see www.clemson.edu/olweus/evidence.html for more information).

Schools are now also gathering data on the use of *OBPP* at the high school level.

A crucial aspect of *OBPP* is that the program requires the involvement of all members of the school community—administrators, teachers, parents, non-teaching staff, and students. Interventions occur at all levels of the school organization (school-level, classroom, and individual).

- **School-level interventions.** Examples of school-level interventions include forming and training a bullying prevention coordinating committee, administering an anonymous survey to determine the extent and types of bullying, developing school-wide rules against bullying, establishing appropriate consequences for students, increasing adult supervision in school hot spots, and developing systematic reporting mechanisms.

- **Classroom activities.** Regular classroom meetings about bullying and peer relationships are designed to improve social relationships and keep teachers in the loop.

- **Individual interventions.** Meetings are conducted between school staff and students who have been bullied, students who are bullying others, and parents of students involved in bullying incidents. School staff members make referrals to community mental health professionals when appropriate.

The *Olweus Bullying Prevention Program* has now been adopted in more than a dozen countries around the world and in thousands of schools in the United States. Clemson University's Institute on Family and Neighborhood Life, guided by Sue Limber, is leading efforts in the United States to implement *OBPP*. Dr. Limber has added two components to the original Olweus model: the developing of school-wide rules and the involvement of community members in the school's antibullying activities.

As you review the goals and objectives of the *Lifelines* program, you will see that they parallel the Olweus model. See Connecting *Lifelines* to the *Olweus Bullying Prevention Program* on the CD-ROM for a more detailed description of how these two programs complement each other.

**10-1**

## WHAT CAN SCHOOLS DO TO HELP SEXUAL MINORITY STUDENTS OVERCOME THE RISK FACTORS THEY FACE AND STRENGTHEN PROTECTIVE FACTORS FOR THEM?

School safety is a critical protective factor against suicidal ideation and attempts for LGBT youth. While not a "program" as such, the Suicide Prevention Resource

Center report, as discussed in chapter 9, recommended a number of strategies to enhance protective factors for LGBT students:

- Institute and enforce policies that prohibit harassment and discrimination and do not tolerate physical violence or harassing language. Comprehensive policies and laws that specifically list personal characteristics, such as sexual orientation and gender identity/expression among others, are the most effective at combating anti-LGBT bullying and harassment.

- Include specific content about the needs of LGBT youth in trainings for staff, teachers, and parents on youth development, mental health issues, gatekeeper skills, and violence prevention.

- Include material on LGBT youth in curricula and resources related to sexuality in the library.

- Integrate specific activities on and for LGBT youth in evidence-based programs that help all youth to develop life skills and critical-thinking skills and to resist violence.

- Provide training for faculty and staff to develop understanding of LGBT youth and children from LGBT families.

- Provide appropriate health care and education. Counselors and health staff need to make their sensitivity to LGBT issues clear.

- Staff members should role-model respectful language, intervene in harassment instances, and bring diverse images into the classroom.

- Provide support for students. Gay-straight alliances are an effective way to help build peer support and acceptance and to promote equality and school change.

*"I transferred into this high school when I was a sophomore and felt really, really alone. In my previous school, I'd known all the kids since elementary school and my sexual orientation was never an issue—I was just one of the crowd. I was really worried that when I got to this new school I'd be ostracized for being gay. I can't describe my relief when I found out there was a gay-straight alliance that met weekly. It made the hardest thing about transferring so much easier."*

—TOBY, AGE NINETEEN

## MY SCHOOL ALREADY HAS SO MANY PROGRAMS. HOW CAN WE DO THEM ALL AND STILL EDUCATE STUDENTS ACADEMICALLY?

Schools have been inundated with separate programs to address specific problem or risk behaviors, including substance abuse, risky sexual behavior, and suicide. However, more comprehensive programs like the ones described in this chapter—programs that promote protective factors such as social problem-solving skills, school connectedness, positive peer relations, and the opportunity to make meaningful contributions—can help prevent a variety of risk behaviors, including substance abuse and suicidal intentions and thoughts. The National Strategy for Suicide Prevention has recommended this more comprehensive approach (SAMHSA 2001).

Another very important thing to keep in mind is that these comprehensive programs also support and enhance students' academic performance, a finding supported by both research and common sense. Students who feel connected and safe at school, who have positive experiences with teachers and peers, who are not sidetracked by substance abuse and other risky behaviors, and who feel valued and important at school are much more able and likely to invest time and effort into their schoolwork and school activities.

## WITH ALL THE BUDGET CUTS MY SCHOOL HAS EXPERIENCED, WE HAVE NO FUNDING FOR EVEN THE BEST PROGRAMS. WE HAVE NO RESOURCES. WHAT CAN *WE* DO?

Don't give up! As long as your school has administrators, faculty, staff, and students, your school has resources. You can still create local programs modeled on the evidence-based strategies presented here. Many statewide and national grant programs support implementing evidence-based, comprehensive programs. An additional strategy is to contact local colleges or universities to see what help they can offer.

## LET'S REVIEW

This manual has tried to present a balanced perspective of intervention techniques for students at risk for suicide. And, while assessment skills are essential for responding to the immediate needs of vulnerable students, this chapter in particular has provided a counterpoint to a focus on a crisis-oriented response to suicide by highlighting ways in which schools can create safety nets for the entire school population. These programs enhance student protections by creating comprehensive and competent communities that provide information, teach skills, enhance feelings of connectedness, and empower all members of the school to play a role in the protection of everyone in the school community.

In closing, we, the authors, want to share an old Irish proverb we learned when teaching the *Lifelines* program to our colleagues in Ireland. It captures the essence of that competent youth suicide prevention community perfectly: *Is ar scáth a chéile a mhaireann na daoine.* Or as we say in English, "It is in the shelter of each other that we live."

## IN YOUR
# Experience...

- What protective factors in your school community encourage feelings of connectedness?
- Can you identify youth who would benefit from some type of peer support programs?
- Off the top of your head, name three trusted adults in your school to whom students turn for help. If you're not one of them, what could you do to be more open to student needs?

## RESOURCES

Black, D. R., N. S. Tobler, and J. P. Sciacca. "Peer Helping/Involvement: An Efficacious Way to Meet the Challenge of Reducing Alcohol, Tobacco, and Other Drug Use among Youth?" *Journal of School Health* 68, no. 3 (1998): 87–93.

Kalafat, J., M. Elias, and M. A. Gara. "The Relationship of Bystander Intervention Variables to Adolescents' Responses to Suicidal Peers." *Journal of Primary Prevention* 13, no. 4 (1993): 231–44.

Kalafat, J., and C. Gagliano. "The Use of Simulations to Assess the Impact of an Adolescent Suicide Response Curriculum." *Suicide and Life-Threatening Behavior* 26, no. 4 (1996): 359–64.

## HANDOUTS

10-1: Connecting *Lifelines* to the *Olweus Bullying Prevention Program*

# References

## Introduction

Granello, D., and P. Granello. 2007. *Suicide: An Essential Guide for Helping Professionals and Educators.* Boston: Pearson Education, Inc.

## Chapter 1

Borowsky, I. W., M. Ireland, and M. D. Resnick. 2001. "Adolescent Suicide Attempts: Risks and Protectors." *Pediatrics* 107 (3): 485–93.

James, B. 1997. "FERPA and School Violence: The Silence That Kills." In *School Violence Intervention: A Practical Handbook,* edited by A.P. Goldstein and J. C. Conoley. New York: Guilford Press.

## Chapter 2

Kalafat, J., and M. Underwood. 1989. *Lifelines: A School-based Adolescent Suicide Response Program.* Dubuque, IA: Kendall-Hunt Publishing.

Shneidman, E. S. 1985. *Definition of Suicide.* New York: John Wiley & Sons.

## Chapter 3

Gair, S., and P. Camilleri. 2000. "Attempted Suicide: Listening to and Learning from Young People." *Queensland Journal of Education Research* 16 (2): 183–206.

## Chapter 4

Beautrais, A. L., D. M. Fergusson, and L. J. Horwood. 2006. "Firearms Legislation and Reductions in Firearm-related Suicide Deaths in New Zealand." *Australian and New Zealand Journal of Psychiatry* 40: 253–59.

Beautrais, A. L., P. R. Joyce, and R. T. Mulder. 1997. "Factors and Life Events in Serious Suicide Attempts among Youth aged 13–24." *Journal of American Academy of Child and Adolescent Psychiatry* 36 (11): 1543–51.

Berman, A. L., D. A. Jobes, and M. M. Silverman. 2006. *Adolescent Suicide: Assessment and Intervention.* Washington, DC: American Psychological Association.

Borowsky, I. W., M. Ireland, and M. D. Resnick. 2001. "Adolescent Suicide Attempts: Risks and Protectors." *Pediatrics* 107 (3): 485–93.

Brent, D.A., M. Baugher, J. Bridge, T. Chen, and L. Chiappetta. 1999. "Age- and Sex-related Risk Factors for Adolescent Suicide." *Journal of the American Academy of Child and Adolescent Psychiatry* 38 (12): 1497–1505.

Centers for Disease Control and Prevention (CDC). 2010a. Web-based Injury Statistics Query and Reporting System (WISQARS) [Online]. National Center for Injury Prevention and Control, CDC (producer). Available at www.cdc.gov/injury/wisqars/index.html.

Centers for Disease Control and Prevention (CDC). 2010b. *Youth Risk Behavior Surveillance—United States, 2009.* Available at www.cdc.gov/mmwr/pdf/ss /ss5905.pdf.

Foley, D., D. Goldston, J. Costello, and A. Angold. 2006. "Proximal Psychiatric Risk Factors for Suicidality in Youth." *Archives of General Psychiatry* 65: 1017–24.

Forman, S. G., and J. Kalafat. 1998. "Substance Abuse and Suicide: Promoting Resilience against Self-destructive Behavior in Youth." *School Psychology Review* 27 (3): 398–406.

Gould, M. S., T. Greenberg, D. M. Velting, and D. Shaffer. 2003. "Youth Suicide Risk and Preventive Interventions: A Review of the Past 10 Years." *Journal of the American Academy of Child & Adolescent Psychiatry* 42 (4): 386.

Gould, M. S., R. King, S. Greenwald, P. Fisher, M. Schwab-Stone, R. Kramer, A. J. Flisher, S. Goodman, G. Canino, and D. Shaffer. 1998. "Psychopathology Associated with Suicidal Ideation and Attempts among Children and Adolescents." *Journal of American Academy of Child and Adolescent Psychiatry* 37 (9): 915–23.

Karch, D. L., L. L. Dahlberg, N. Patel, T. W. Davis, J. E. Logan, H. A. Hill, and L. Ortega. 2009. *Surveillance for Violent Deaths—National Violent Death Reporting System, 16 States, 2006.* MMWR, 58 (SS01), 1–44.

Resnick, M. D., P. S. Bearman, R. W. Blum, K. E. Bauman, K. M. Harris, J. Jones, J. Tabor, T. Beuhring, R. E. Sieving, M. Shew, M. Ireland, L. H. Bearinger, and J. R. Udry. 1997. "Protecting Adolescents from Harm: Findings from the National Longitudinal Study of Adolescent Health." *Journal of the American Medical Association* 278 (10): 823–32.

Scott, M. A., H. C. Wilcox, I. Schonfeld, M. Davies, R. C. Hicks, J. Turner, and D. Shaffer. 2009. "School-based Screening to Identify At-Risk Students Not Already Known to School Professionals: The Columbia Suicide Screen." *American Journal of Public Health* 99 (2): 324–29.

Scott, M., H. Wilcox, Y. Huo, J. Turner, P. Fisher, and D. Shaffer. 2010. "School-based Screening for Suicide Risk: Balancing Costs and Benefits." *American Journal of Public Health* 100 (9): 1648–52.

Shaffer, D., M. S. Gould, P. Fisher, P. Trautman, D. Moreau, M. Kleinman, and M. Flory. 1996. "Psychiatric Diagnoses in Child and Adolescent Suicide." *Archives of General Psychiatry* 53 (4): 339–48.

Shaffer, D., M. Scott, H. Wilcox, C. Maslow, R. Hicks, C. P. Lucas, R. Garfinkel, and S. Greenwald. 2004. "The Columbia Suicide Screen: Validity and Reliability of a Screen for Youth Suicide and Depression." *Journal of the American Academy of Child and Adolescent Psychiatry* 43 (1): 71–79.

Zayas, L., L. E. Gulbas, N. Fedoravicius, and L. J. Cabassa. 2010. "Patterns of Distress, Precipitating Events, and Reflections on Suicide Attempts by Young Latinas." *Social Science & Medicine* 70 (11): 1773–79.

## Chapter 9

Almeida, J., R. M. Johnson, H. L. Corliss, B. E. Molnar, and D. Azrael. 2009. "Emotional Distress among LGBT Youth: The Influence of Perceived Discrimination Based on Sexual Orientation." *Journal of Youth and Adolescence* 38 (7): 1001–14.

Arsenealt, L., L. Bowes, and S. Shakoor. 2010. "Bullying Victimization in Youth and Mental Problems: 'Much Ado about Nothing'?" *Psychological Medicine* 40 (5): 717–29.

Benard, B., and K. Marshall. 2001. *Protective Factors in Individuals, Families, and Schools: National Longitudinal Study on Adolescent Health Findings.* (Resilience Research for Prevention Programs.) Anoka, MN: Central Center for the Application of Prevention Technologies.

Birkett, M., D. Espelage, and B. Koenig. 2009. "LGB and Questioning Students in Schools: The Moderating Effects of Homophobic Bullying and School Climate on Negative Outcomes." *Journal of Youth and Adolescence* 38 (7): 989–1000.

Daniel, S. S., A. K. Walsh, D. B. Goldston, E. M. Arnold, B. A. Reboussin, and F. B. Wood. 2006. "Suicidality, School Dropout, and Reading Problems among Adolescents." *Journal of Learning Disabilities* 39 (6): 507–14.

D'Augelli, A. R., A. H. Grossman, N. P. Salter, J. J. Vasey, M. T. Starks, and K. A. Sinclair. 2005. "Predicting the Suicide Attempts of Lesbian, Gay, and Bisexual Youth." *Suicide and Life-Threatening Behavior* 35 (6): 646–60.

Finkelhor, D., H. Turner, R. Ormrod, S. Hamby, and K. Kracke. 2009. *Children's Exposure to Violence: A Comprehensive National Survey.* NCJ 227744. Rockville, MD: U.S. Department of Justice, Office of Juvenile Justice and Delinquency Prevention.

Hindujua, S., and J. W. Patchin. 2010. "Bullying, Cyberbullying, and Suicide." *Archives of Suicide Research* 14 (3): 206–21.

Neihart, M. and R. Olenchak. 2002. "Creatively Gifted Children." In *The Social and Emotional Development of Gifted Children,* edited by M. Neihart, S. Reis, N. Robinson, and S. Moon. Washington, DC: National Association for Gifted Children.

Olweus, D. 1993. *Bullying at School: What We Know and What We Can Do.* New York: Blackwell.

Olweus, D., S. Limber, and S. Mihalic. 1999. *The Bullying Prevention Program: Blueprints for Violence Prevention.* Boulder, CO: Center for the Study and Prevention of Violence.

Orpinas, P., and A. M. Horne. 2006. *Bullying Prevention: Creating a Positive School Climate and Developing Social Competence.* Washington, DC: American Psychological Association.

Resnick, M. D., P. S. Bearman, R. W. Blum, K. E. Bauman, K. M. Harris, J. Jones, J. Tabor, T. Beuhring, R. E. Sieving, M. Shew, M. Ireland, L. H. Bearinger, and J. R. Udry. 1997. "Protecting Adolescents from Harm: Findings from the National Longitudinal Study on Adolescent Health." *Journal of the American Medical Association* 278 (10): 823–32.

Rose, C. A., L. E. Monda-Amaya, and D. L. Espelage. 2010. "Bullying Perpetration and Victimization in Special Education: A Review of the Literature." *Remedial and Special Education.* Published online February 18, 2010.

Russell, S. T., and K. Joyner. 2001. "Adolescent Sexual Orientation and Suicide Risk: Evidence from a National Study." *American Journal of Public Health* 91 (8): 1276–81.

Saewyc, E. M., Y. Homma, C. L. Skay, L. H. Bearinger, M. D. Resnick, and E. Reis. 2009. "Protective Factors in the Lives of Bisexual Adolescents in North America." *American Journal of Public Health* 99 (1): 110–17.

Seattle Teen Health Survey. 1999. Seattle Public Schools and the U.S. Centers for Disease Control and Prevention.

Suicide Prevention Resource Center. 2008. *Suicide Risk and Prevention for Lesbian, Gay, Bisexual, and Transgender Youth.* Newton, MA: Education Development Center.

Suicide Prevention Resource Center. 2010. *Suicide Prevention among Lesbian, Gay, Bisexual, and Transgender Youth: A Workshop for Professionals Who Serve Youth.* Newton, MA: Education Development Center.

Swearer, S. 2010. "Bullying: What Parents, Teachers Can Do to Stop It." Newswise: American Psychological Association. www.newswise.com/articles /bullying-what-parents-teachers-can-do-to-stop-it.

Thomas, V., K. E. Ray, and S. M. Moon. 2007. "Counseling Gifted Individuals and Their Families: A Systems Perspective." In *Counseling the Gifted,* edited by S. Mendaglio and J. Peterson, 29–95. Waco, TX: Prufrock Press.

Wang, J., R. J. Iannotti, and T. R. Nansel. 2009. "School Bullying among Adolescents in the United States: Physical, Verbal, Relational, and Cyber." *Journal of Adolescent Health* 45 (4): 368–75.

## Chapter 10

Benard, B. 1991. *Fostering Resiliency in Kids: Protective Factors in the Family, School and Community.* Portland, OR: Northwest Regional Educational Laboratory.

Benard, B. 2004. *Turning the Corner: From Risk to Resilience.* Minneapolis: National Resilience Resource Center, University of Minnesota.

Borowsky, I. W., M. Ireland, and M. D. Resnick. 2001. "Adolescent Suicide Attempts: Risks and Protectors." *Pediatrics* 107 (3): 485–93.

Fleming, M., and K. Towey, eds. 2002. *Educational Forum on Adolescent Health: Youth Bullying, May.* Chicago: American Medical Association.

Johnson, D. W. 1996. "Conflict Resolution and Peer Mediation Programs in Elementary and Secondary Schools." *Review of Educational Research* 66 (4): 459–506.

Kalafat, J. 2003. "School Approaches to Youth Suicide Prevention." *American Behavioral Scientist* 46 (9): 1211–23.

Kalafat, J., and M. Elias. 1992. "Adolescents' Experience with Response to Suicidal Peers." *Suicide and Life-Threatening Behavior* 22 (3): 315–21.

Kalafat, J., and D. M. Ryerson. "The Implementation and Institutionalization of a School-based Youth Suicide Prevention Program." *Journal of Primary Prevention* 19, no. 3 (1999): 157–75.

Orpinas, P., and A. M. Horne. 2006. *Bullying Prevention: Creating a Positive School Climate and Developing Social Competence.* Washington, DC: American Psychological Association.

Resnick, M. D., P. S. Bearman, R. W. Blum, K. E. Bauman, K. M. Harris, J. Jones, J. Tabor, T. Beuhring, R. E. Sieving, M. Shew, M. Ireland, L. H. Bearinger, and J. R. Udry. 1997. "Protecting Adolescents from Harm: Findings from the National Longitudinal Study on Adolescent Health." *Journal of the American Medical Association* 278 (10): 823–32.

SAMHSA. 2001. *National Strategy for Suicide Prevention: Goals and Objectives for Action.* Pub id: SMA01-3517. Rockville, MD: U.S. Department of Health and Human Services.

Suicide Prevention Resource Center. 2008. *Suicide Risk and Prevention for Lesbian, Gay, Bisexual, and Transgender Youth.* Newton, MA: Education Development Center.

Wyman, P. A., C. H. Brown, M. LoMurray, K. Schmeelk-Cone, M. Petrova, Q. Yu, E. Walsh, X. Tu, and W. Wang. 2010. "An Outcome Evaluation of the Sources of Strength Suicide Prevention Program Delivered by Adolescent Peer Leaders in High Schools." *American Journal of Public Health* 100 (9): 1653–61.

# About the Authors

........................................................................................

## Maureen M. Underwood, L.C.S.W.

Maureen Underwood is a licensed clinical social worker and certified group psychotherapist with over thirty years of experience in mental health and crisis intervention. With a practice specialty in grief, trauma, and crisis resolution for children and families, she has developed numerous programs and published extensively on these and other related topics. From 1985 to 2000, she was the coordinator of the New Jersey Adolescent Suicide Prevention Project. In this role she initiated collaborative relationships between mental health and educational systems statewide, providing in-service training, consultation on policy development, and assistance in the implementation of procedures for school-based crisis management. She is the co-author of *Managing Sudden Traumatic Loss in the Schools* and *Beyond 9/11: Helping School Staff Prepare for the 9/11 Anniversary.* She is also the author of the National Association of Social Work's policy statement on adolescent suicide and was a charter member of the New Jersey Governor's Council on Youth Suicide Prevention.

Her most current work focuses on school youth suicide awareness programs. As clinical director of the Society for the Prevention of Teen Suicide, she has developed an online interactive training program for educators in suicide awareness that has received a best-practice designation from the Suicide Prevention Resource Center. She is a nationally certified trainer for the Suicide Prevention Resource Center's Clinical Assessment and Management of Suicide Risk training protocol. She is also the co-author of *Lifelines: A Suicide Prevention Program* and *Lifelines Postvention: Responding to Suicide and Other Traumatic Death,* which are available through Hazelden Publications.

Maureen maintains a private psychotherapy practice in Morristown, New Jersey.

## Judith Springer, Psy.D.

Judith Springer, Psy.D., is a licensed psychologist and a certified school psychologist with several decades of experience working in and with schools, universities, and other organizations. The guiding purpose of Judith's life and work experience has been her desire to help individuals develop emotional intelligence skills and to aid them in creating effective groups with a genuine sense of community. This focus has been reflected across a variety of settings: fifth grade teacher and reading teacher in urban and suburban schools; crisis counselor and peer program advisor in a public high school; co-founder of Youth Empowerment of Youth Empowerment Strategies, Inc., a human relations training company; co-founder and co-director of Anytown, New Jersey, a teen leadership and prejudice prevention program; former faculty member of the Graduate School of Applied and Professional Psychology (GSAPP) at Rutgers University; a licensed psychologist in private practice in Morristown, New Jersey; co-founder and program director of the Ceceilyn Miller Institute for Leadership and Diversity (CMI), a non-profit human relations training organization; and a board member of the Society for the Prevention of Teen Suicide.

## Michelle Ann-Rish Scott, M.S.W., Ph.D.

Michelle Scott is an assistant professor at Monmouth University's School of Social Work in West Long Branch, New Jersey, and an adjunct professor at Columbia University: College of Physicians and Surgeon's Department of Child and Adolescent Psychiatry in New York, New York. She is an accomplished researcher in the area of adolescent suicide prevention and school-based screening for suicide risk. She has published in various journals such as the *Journal of the American Academy of Child and Adolescent Psychiatry* as well as the *American Journal of Public Health*. Her other areas of interest include translational research for adolescent depression and suicide prevention (i.e. moving programming to evidence-based and evidence-based programs to practice), juvenile justice, adolescent alcohol use, and mental health service utilization.

She currently teaches research and statistics to up-and-coming social workers in the BSW and MSW programs at Monmouth University, West Long Branch, New Jersey.